Springer
Tokyo
Berlin
Heidelberg
New York
Hong Kong
London
Milan
Paris

M. Hatanaka, H. Yamada

Co-trending:

A Statistical System Analysis of Economic Trends

Springer

Michio Hatanaka
Professor Emeritus, Osaka University
1-30-12 Kichijoji Kita-machi, Musashino
Tokyo 180-0001, Japan

Hiroshi Yamada
Associate Professor, Faculty of Economics, Hiroshima University
1-2-1 Kagamiyama, Higashi-Hiroshima
Hiroshima 739-8525, Japan

Publication of this book was supported by a Grant-in-Aid from the Zengin Foundation for Studies on Economics and Finance.

ISBN 978-4-431-65914-3   ISBN 978-4-431-65912-9 (eBook)
DOI 10.1007/978-4-431-65912-9
Library of Congress Cataloging-in-Publication Data

Hatanaka, Michio.
Co-trending : a statistical system analysis of economic trends / M. Hatanaka, H. Yamada.
p. cm.
Includes bibliographical references.

1. Econometrics. 2. Cointegration. 3. Economic forecasting--Statistical methods. 4. Japan--Economic conditions--1945---Econometric models. I. Yamada, H. (Hiroshi), 1967- II. Title.

HB139.H378 2003
330'.01'5195--dc22

Printed on acid-free paper

Softcover reprint of the hardcover 1st edition 2003

Typesetting: Authors

SPIN: 10932346

Preface

In this book new econometric methods are developed to investigate the relations among deterministic trend components in different variables. Needs for such methods have seldom been appreciated in macroeconometrics, but we believe that they contribute to analyses of the unique history of the Japanese macroeconomy since World War II. As is well known, the growth rate has declined through this period. However the decline has not been steady, but concentrated in two periods: 1971-73 and 1990-92. In other words, the deterministic trends in logarithmic scales are not linear, but subjected to structural changes that occurred in these two periods. How such trends could have been generated is an intriguing question. If economic hypotheses are provided with intelligent insight, the reality of such hypotheses can be examined by our econometric methods, contributing to finding answers to this question.

The book is entitled co-trending because we have adapted the conceptual framework of cointegration for our analysis of deterministic trends. In Chapter 2 we have defined the co-trending rank, r, in two versions of framework. In the first version no specific functions of time are assumed on the deterministic trends, and the orders of trends expressed by power functions of sample size are compared between the original variables and their linear combinations. This version is called the non-parametric approach. In the second version we presuppose a model that generates piecewise linear functions of time, possibly with rank default, and the co-trending rank is defined as the rank of a certain matrix parameter. This version is called the parametric approach. Chapter 3 develops asymptotic analyses on principal components of the data covariance matrix of original n variables. The non-parametric approach is sufficient for this purpose. It has been found necessary to pay our attention not only to the co-trending rank, but also to the dimension of the space that consists of vectors that are both a co-trending vector and a cointegration vector. This dimension is denoted by r_1. Given r and r_1, the n principal components are classified into three classes that consist of $n - r$, $r - r_1$, and r_1 components, respectively. Each class has a distinctive, statistical characteristic. Our strategy is to determine r and r_1 by testing these characteristics. Though it will be fully developed in Chapters 4 through 6, it will also be previewed at the end of Chapter 3. In Chapter 4 the results from Chapter 3 are transferred on the parametric approach in order to implement such statistical tests. Chapter 5 shows how a different set of r and r_1 produces different results of unit root tests applied to n principal components. Similar investigations are made on trend tests in Chapter 6. In Chapter 7 we assemble all the results of tests to determine r and r_1 jointly from the n principal components. In Chapter 8 results of simulation studies are presented to investigate the finite sample performance of the method. An application to a simple set of Japanese data is also shown there. All the mathematical proofs are collected in Appendix A. Given r and r_1 Appendix B shows how to perform statistical inference on the co-trending matrix. The relations among the trend components of different variables are closely associated with the relations among their structural changes, which will be called the co-breaking. It will be briefly discussed in Section 2.4 of Chapter 2, and more fully in Appendix C.

The first author began research on deterministic trends in 1995. A number of approaches have been explored, and some have been published. All of them are superseded by the present book. He is grateful to Naoto Kunitomo and Mitsuo Saito, who called his attention to this research topic, and Mitsuhiro Odaki and Kazuo Yamada, who helped his work at the earlier stages prior to this book. The second author thanks the Ministry of Education, Culture, Sports, Science and Technology for research support under Grant-in-Aid no. 14730026. The authors are grateful to grant for publication from the Zengin Foundation for Studies in Economics and Finance, and to Springer-Verlag for support throughout this project.

June 2003

Michio Hatanaka
Hiroshi Yamada

Contents

1 Introduction

To invite the readers to the present book we begin Section 1.1 with what has motivated the authors to study the relations among deterministic trends. The rest of this section consists of an expository explanation of co-trending and presentation of highlights of the authors' results. In Section 1.2 the literature on the relations among trends will be reviewed. We have explored a number of different approaches before settling on the one in this book, and they are discussed briefly in Section 1.3. The mathematical notations are assembled in Section 1.4.

1.1 Motivation and Results of the Research

The current econometric practice on time series data can be summarised as follows. All the variables are initially detrended, and then the residuals in different variables are related to each other. Even the practices that do not appear to adopt this procedure are in fact equivalent to it. Practitioners must believe that *the trends do not*, but *the residuals do* provide information useful for economic studies.

The practice may well be justified if the deterministic trends are linear functions of time in all the variables. If each of n variables has a linear trend with possibly different slope coefficients, there must necessarily be $n - 1$ linear relations among these trends, and the vector of coefficients in each relation can be determined purely mathematically from the n slope coefficients. Such relations among n trends rarely offer information useful for economics. On the other hand the residuals can be interpreted as business cycles, and the relations among the business cycles of different variables are hoped to provide information useful for economics.

Let us investigate trends in economic time series data to see if they are linear. Figure 1.1 presents in logarithmic scales the seasonally adjusted, quarterly data of real GDP in Japan, the UK, and the USA from 1957 to 2000. A linear trend is fitted in each case. One important criterion to judge the adequacy of fit is that the discrepancy between the data and the linear trend should be primarily a realisation of a

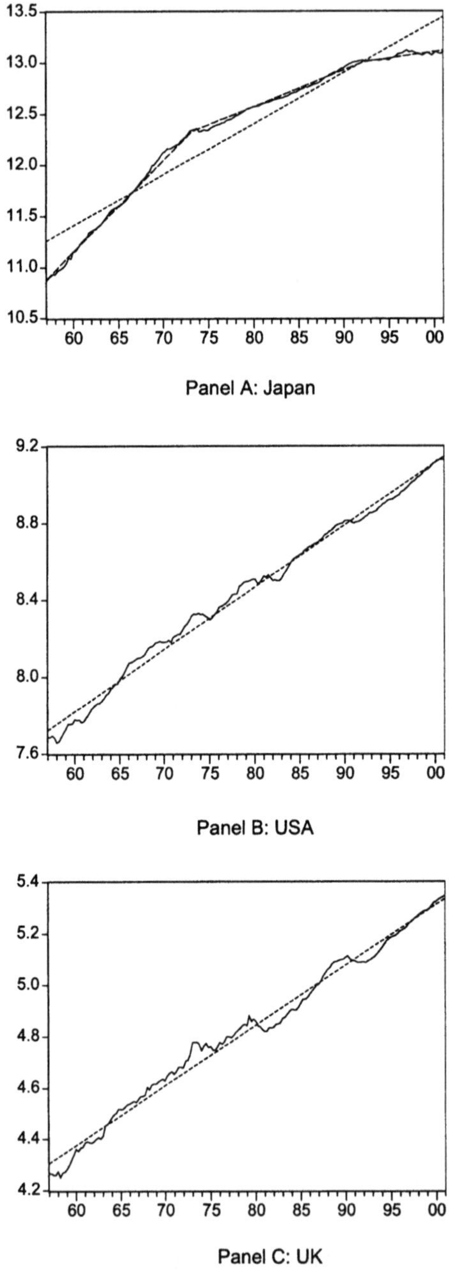

Figure 1.1. ln(real GDP), 1957(I)-2001(I)

stochastic variable that represents business cycles. It seems to be generally accepted in empirical studies on the UK and the USA that the linear trends are adequate. As for Japan, the discrepancy from the linear trend lacks the oscillations that could be accounted for as business cycles. Indeed, the opinion common among macroeconomists is that structural changes in Japanese growth rates possibly occurred in two steps, one about 1971-73, and the other about 1990-92. The piecewise linear line on the Japanese series in Figure 1.1 shows a trend with two break points, one chosen within each of the two periods. (The time point at which a structural change occurs is called a break point in the current econometric terminology.) The discrepancy of the real data from this deterministic trend involves more oscillations that may be regarded business cycles. (It is also seen that a quadratic trend does not fit the Japanese real GDP well.) Many macroeconomic time series in Japan other than the real GDP also involve trends that are more complicated than simple linear. We have encountered a similar case on Brazilian data.

When we deal with the variables in which deterministic trends are more complicated than a simple linear form, the relations among trends of different variables may well deserve a serious investigation. To explain this point we shall use a simple example of two variables without claiming its importance in growth economics. Figure 1.2 presents in natural logarithms the quarterly, seasonally adjusted real GDP and nominal money supply, (M2+CD), both in Japan, over the period from 1980(I) to 2001(III). The sources of data of the two series are independent. Nevertheless the following observations seem quite plausible. (i) The trends of both variables can be represented by piecewise linear functions of time. (ii) The break points of trends of two variables are located at about the same time point. (iii) However the slopes of trends are different between the two variables.

These observations lead to a series of interesting questions. (i) Is there a linear relation between the trends of two variables? If the ratios of slopes of two variables are identical between the periods before and after the break point, the trends of two variables would be linearly related throughout the sample period. (ii) If there exists a linear relation, how could it be generated? (iii) Is this relation identical to the relation between the business cycles of the two variables?

Our book investigates statistical aspects of these questions, namely (i) and (iii); (ii) has to be answered by economic hypotheses provided by macroeconomics. However, empirical plausibility of the hypotheses has to be examined with the statistical evidence obtained from answers to the questions (i) and (iii).

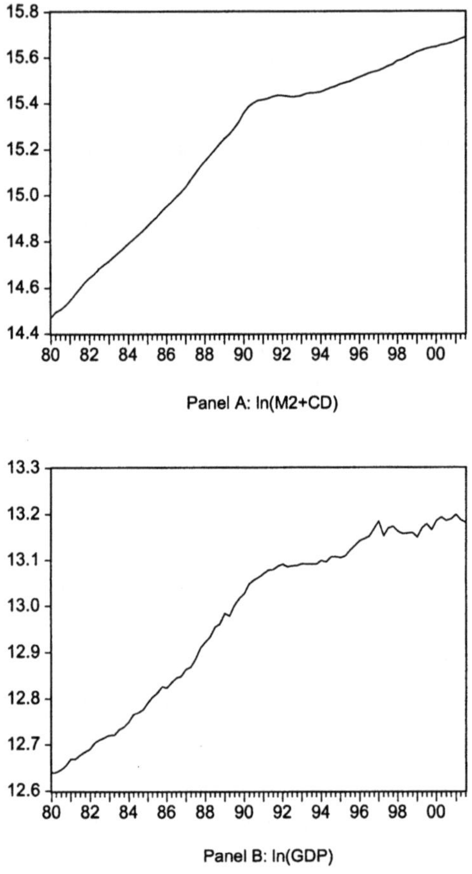

Figure 1.2. Japanese ln(real GDP) and ln(M2+CD), 1980(I)-2001(III)

We shall adopt the conceptual framework of cointegration developed for a multivariate stochastic process in Granger (1981) and Engle and Granger (1987). A set of I(1) variables are said to be cointegrated if a linear combination of the variables is I(0). The vector of weights in such a combination is a cointegration vector. The cointegration rank is said to be r, if there exist r linearly independent cointegration vectors but there cannot be more. The cointegration approach examines reality of existence of a set of relations, which should be contrasted to some other econometric methodology where existence of certain relations is simply assumed.

In our book the trends in a set of n variables are piecewise linear functions of time, sharing the same set of break points within the sample period. A simple linear trend is included as a special case of the piecewise linear trend. As regards the relations among the deterministic trends, we say that the set of n variables are *co-trended* if a linear combination of the variables does not have a piecewise linear trend. The vector of weights in such a combination is a co-trending vector. The co-trending rank is r, if there exist r linearly independent co-trending vectors but there cannot be more. The co-trending rank is the number of linear relations that hold among the deterministic trends of n variables. In our book we shall present a method to determine the co-trending rank from the original time series data of n variables. In some cases the co-trending rank directly restricts the range of economic hypotheses consistent with observations. Moreover, with a given co-trending rank it is possible to perform statistical inference on the co-trending vectors, which further constrains the range of economic hypotheses.

We shall go further by assuming that the stochastic parts of n variables are I(1) but possibly cointegrated. Among the r co-trending vectors mentioned above, some may also be a cointegration vector in the sense that it belongs to the linear vector subspace of cointegration vectors on the stochastic parts of the n variables. Such a co-trending vector represents not only a relation among the trends, but also a relation among the strictly I(1) stochastic portions of the variables. Suppose that r_1 but not more of co-trending vectors are cointegration vectors. We shall determine this number, r_1. The current macroeconomic theories offer little to determine whether the co-trending and the cointegration vectors differ or not, but this determination is important not only to study the mechanism of economic growth, but also to implement the statistical inference on the co-trending and the cointegration vectors.

1.2 Review of the Literature

We have found that the literature on the relations among deterministic trends is surprisingly scarce. Klein and Kosobud (1961) built a simultaneous equations model of economic growth on the basis of trends of relevant variables. We are concerned with a VAR-type approach in this book. Granger (1986) proposed a model for a set of variables in which the identical relationship held among their deterministic trends and among their stochastic I(1) trends, and Granger (1988) suggested to use this information to estimate the deterministic trends. Ogaki and Park (1998), which was available in 1988, pointed out that the relations among deterministic trends might be different from those among stochastic trends. A model in Johansen (1994) for a linear trend and a model in Johansen et al. (2000) for trends with structural breaks did allow the relations among deterministic trends to be different from the relations among stochastic trends. These studies are for the analyses of stochastic trends rather than of deterministic trends. On the basis of unit root tests on some Japanese time series, Kunitomo (1996) argued that macroeconomic relations in Japan should be considered as the relations among deterministic trend parts of relevant variables. The co-breaking in Hendry and Mizon (1998) and Clements and Hendry (1999) is certainly related to our motivation. However, ours is co-trending and these are not identical, as will be shown later in Chapter 2. Hatanaka (1998) pointed out by an example regarding the neutrality of money hypothesis that the number of relations among deterministic trends of different variables played an important role in formulating testable hypotheses, and also in implementing tests on the relations among deterministic trends.

1.3 Exploration of Different Approaches

There are two possible approaches to determine the co-trending rank. One is the parametric approach and the other is the non-parametric approach. In the parametric approach, trends in different variables are constructed by some linear combination of elementary trend functions of time. A list of elementary trend functions must be provided, and it requires information on where the break points are. On the other hand, in the non-parametric approach, the elementary trend functions are not used, and it means that the functional forms of trends could be left completely free. If the list of elementary trend functions can be chosen appropriately, the parametric approach would be superior to the non-parametric approach, but the selection of elementary trend functions might pose a difficulty in practice. A non-parametric approach to the determination of co-trending rank was adopted in Hatanaka (2000), but studies of decision rules were left incomplete there. In this book, we will determine the co-trending rank on the parametric approach, although some basic theoretical analyses on the non-parametric approach will be discussed in Chapters 2 and 3.

The parametric approach may be implemented by either the full-fledged maximum likelihood method or ad hoc methods. The maximum likelihood method requires complete specification of the entire model covering both the stochastic and the deterministic parts of the variables. We have thought that the co-trending rank and the cointegration rank are difficult to determine *jointly* in the likelihood approach. As for the ad hoc methods, we have investigated the statistics associated with the data covariance matrix and also the reduced rank regression on the list of elementary trend functions. Moreover, either the eigenvalues or the principal components may be considered with respect to the data covariance matrix. Hatanaka (2000) shows that the eigenvalues lead to a certain decision rule to determine the co-trending rank, but the distribution to be used for the inference contains many nuisance parameters, in which some consistent estimates have to be substituted. The method in this book relies primarily on the principal components, while giving the reduced rank regression a subsidiary role.

1.4 Notations

The following notations will be used. Let d be a real number. $[d]$ denotes the integer part of d. Let D be a $T \times k$ matrix. det$[D]$ denotes the determinant of the matrix D. csp(D) and rank(D) denote respectively the column space and the rank of the matrix D. $\boldsymbol{P}(D)$ denotes the projection matrix on csp(D), i.e., $\boldsymbol{P}(D) = D(D'D)^{-}D$, where $(D'D)^{-}$ denotes the generalised inverse of the matrix $D'D$. S is the $T \times T$ lower triangular matrix of which all the elements in the lower triangle are 1. The matrix S is used to construct time series of partial sums. Let y be a column vector of T elements. We shall say that y is $O(T^{-c})$ as $T \to \infty$ (or $O_p(T^{-c})$ for a stochastic y) when $\| y \|$ is $O(T^{-c})$ (or $O_p(T^{-c})$). Similarly for $o(T^{-c})$ (or $o_p(T-c)$). Let Y be a $T \times k$ matrix, where k is fixed while $T \to \infty$. We shall say that Y is $O(T^{-c})$ (or $O_p(T^{-c})$ if $Y\gamma$ is $O(T^{-c})$ (or $O_p(T^{-c})$) for any non-stochastic γ ($\neq 0$). The meaning of "not $o(1)$" or "not $o_p(1)$" is clear when it refers to a vector y, but could be confusing about a matrix Y. This statement will be restricted to a vector y. Δ signifies the difference operator. It will also be used to denote the $(T-1) \times T$ matrix such that ΔX is the data matrix of the series of Δx_t if X is the data matrix of the series of x_t.

2 Co-trending

Our basic research strategy is to model the relations among deterministic trends directly without using the parameters of stochastic parts of models. Direct modelling is divided into the parametric approach and the non-parametric approach. The parametric approach is based on a list of parametrically specified functions of time, which will be called trend functions, while the non-parametric approach does not use such functions. We begin with the non-parametric approach in Section 2.1, which will then be followed by the parametric approach in Section 2.2. Section 2.3 will present an example of trend functions that is hoped will be useful for empirical studies of the Japanese economy. Section 2.4 will compare our co-trending with the co-breaking in Hendry and Mizon (1998) and Clements and Hendry (1999). Section 2.5 will briefly survey the history of the direct modelling and the indirect modelling in the time series analyses. We had long seen the indirect modelling only, but Schmidt and Phillips (1992) have advocated the direct modelling.

We suppose that n-variate time series $x_t = [x_{1t}, \ldots, x_{nt}]'$ is generated by the following model:

$$x_t = d_t + s_t, \quad t = 1, \ldots, T, \tag{2.1}$$

where $d_t = [d_{1t}, \ldots, d_{nt}]'$ is non-stochastic, $s_t = [s_{1t}, \ldots, s_{nt}]'$ is stochastic with mean zero, and neither d_t nor s_t is observable. Define $X' = [x_1, \ldots, x_T]$, $X'_D = [d_1, \ldots, d_T]$, and $X'_S = [s_1, \ldots, s_T]$. Then, (2.1) can be represented as

$$X = X_D + X_S, \tag{2.2}$$

where $\mathrm{E}(X_S) = 0$, and $\mathrm{E}(X) = X_D$.

Most of existing econometric studies have been concerned with X_S, and X_D has been investigated in order to make studies of X_S more accurate. Unlike these studies, we focus our attention on the structure of deterministic component X_D, and to accomplish the aim, X_D will be modelled directly without using the parameters of models of X_S.

2.1 Co-trending in the Non-parametric Approach

Co-trending may be formulated as follows:

Assumption 2.1 *(i) We assume that each column of X_D is $O(T^{3/2})$ and at least one column of X_D is not $o(T^{3/2})$. (ii) Let B be an $n \times r$ full column rank matrix and let $B_\perp$ be an orthogonal complement matrix of B. We assume (a) that $X_D B$ is $O(T^{1/2})$ and (b) that $X_D B_\perp \delta$ is not $o(T^{3/2})$ for an arbitrary $(n-r)$-dimensional non-zero column vector δ.*

The co-trending postulated in Assumption 2.1 is regarded as non-parametric because they involve only the orders as $T \to \infty$. Under the assumption the number of relations among deterministic trends is r, and the coefficient matrix of the relations is B.

Definition 2.1 *We define that matrix B that satisfies Assumption 2.1 is a co-trending matrix. We also define that the rank of the matrix, which is denoted by r, is co-trending rank.*

As in the case of cointegration, $X_D B_\perp$ may be interpreted as common deterministic trends. This implies that the number of common deterministic trends are $n - r$, and they are allocated among n variables. Assumption 2.1(ii)(a) and the latter part of (i) preclude the case where $r = n$. On the other hand, we allow $r = 0$, in which case B does not exist and in this sense they are not co-trended. In Assumption 2.1(ii)(a) we did not impose a stronger condition, $X_D B = 0$, so that the relations may have residuals, of which the order is $O(T^{1/2})$. The mean of residuals may not be zero. If the residuals should have zero means, X_D in Assumption 2.1 should be replaced by $(I - \boldsymbol{P}(\boldsymbol{\iota}))X_D$, where $\boldsymbol{\iota}$ is $T \times 1$ vector of one. We allow one column of the matrix B being a unit vector when a column of X_D is $O(T^{1/2})$, although in this case the co-trending relation is trivial. If all n variables have a linear trend, i.e., each column of X_D is a scalar multiple of $\boldsymbol{t} = [1, \ldots, T]'$, which is $O(T^{3/2})$, then r is $n - 1$. This is a relatively uninteresting case. We have confined our consideration to the trends in $O(T^{3/2})$, thus quadratic or even higher order trends are excluded. It is noteworthy, however, that it is possible to extend our framework. For example, trends in $O(T^{5/2})$ can be incorporated as follows: Suppose that $\mathrm{csp}([B_*, B_{*\perp}])$ is the whole n-dimensional space, $X_D B_*$ is $O(T^{3/2})$, while $X_D B_{*\perp}\delta$ is not $o(T^{5/2})$ for any δ. Next, $\mathrm{csp}(B_*)$ is written as $\mathrm{csp}([B, B_\perp])$, to which Assumption 2.1 is applied. However, we shall not pursue this line in this book.

2.2 Co-trending in the Parametric Approach

In order to model X_D parametrically, we introduce here the elementary function matrix, $H_T' = [h_{T,1}, \ldots, h_{T,T}]$, where $h_{T,t}$ is a nonstochastic p-dimensional column vector.

Definition 2.2 *H_T is an elementary function matrix if (i) it contains no unknown parameters, (ii) $p \geq n - r$, (iii) regarding H_T,*

$$[T^{-1/2}H_T, T^{-3/2}SH_T]'[T^{-1/2}H_T, T^{-3/2}SH_T] \tag{2.3}$$

converges to a nonsingular matrix as $T \to \infty$, and (iv) regarding ΔH_T, the number of rows of ΔH_T which are not zero remains bounded while $T \to \infty$, and so do the norms of such rows.

The simplest example of a column of H_T is $\boldsymbol{\iota}$. As for Definition 2.2(iv), all elements of $\Delta\boldsymbol{\iota}$ are zero for all T. Another example is the following step function, which has been used to represent structural changes in deterministic trends in unit root tests since Perron (1989). Let b denote a scalar, known parameter such that $1 > b > 0$. Construct

$$du_T(t, b) = \begin{cases} 0 & \text{if } t \leq [Tb] \\ 1 & \text{if } t > [Tb]. \end{cases}$$

Here b and $[Tb]$ are called respectively break fraction and break point. The following column vector

$$\boldsymbol{du}(b) = [du_T(1, b), \ldots, du_T(T, b)]' \tag{2.4}$$

can be a column of H_T.

The number of elementary functions is p, and Definition 2.2(ii) states that p should not be less than the number of common trends. Noting that the task in this book is to determine the co-trending rank r and that r is determined if and only if $n-r$ is determined, the readers would wonder how Definition 2.2(ii) can be guaranteed. We shall return to this problem at the end of the present subsection. Equation (2.3) implies that H_T is $O(T^{1/2})$ and that SH_T is $O(T^{3/2})$.

Definition 2.3 *SH_T is a elementary trend function matrix if H_T is a elementary function matrix.*

Given r, $1 \leq r < n$, the series of d_t in (2.1) will be constructed from the series of $h_{T,t}$ so that the number of common trends in X_D is $n - r$. We shall use the device which Johansen (1988) originated to investigate interrelated stochastic trends. Five matrices, F, B, $F_\perp$, $B_\perp$, and M are introduced. Both F and B are $n \times r$ full column rank matrices. $F_\perp$ ($B_\perp$) is an orthogonal complement matrix of F (B) and M is $n \times p$. For the time being B and $B_\perp$ here have nothing to do with the B and $B_\perp$ in Assumption 2.1, but the reason to use B and $B_\perp$ will be made clear later. A square matrix, A, will be said to be stable if and only if all roots of $\det[I - A\lambda] = 0$ are outside the unit circle of the complex plane. This language is justified by the well-known result that the difference equation, $x_t - Ax_{t-1} = 0$, satisfies the stability condition if and only if all roots of $\det[I - A\lambda] = 0$ are outside the unit circle. Also the roots that lie outside the unit circle will be said to be stable.

Assumption 2.2 *The time series of d_t in* (2.1) *is generated by*

$$\Delta d_t = FB'd_{t-1} + Mh_{T,t}, \quad t = 1, \ldots, T, \tag{2.5}$$

with $d_0 = 0$, where F and B are such that $(I_r + B'F)$ is stable, $\operatorname{rank}(M'F_\perp) = n - r$, *and $H_T' = [h_{T,1}, \ldots, h_{T,T}]$ is an elementary function matrix.*

Lemma 2.1 *If $(I_r + B'F)$ is stable, the following two conditions hold: (i) The roots of* $\det[I_n - (I_n + FB')\lambda] = 0$ *consist of (real) unit roots with multiplicity, $n - r$, and r stable roots. (ii) The matrices $B'F$, $F_\perp' B_\perp$, $[F, B_\perp]$, and $[B, F_\perp]$ are nonsingular.*

Toda (1994) used the lemma above for his simulation study of cointegration. Since the homogeneous part of the difference equation, (2.5), is $d_t - (I_n + FB')d_{t-1}$, Lemma 2.1(i) suggests that the sequence of d_t contains $n - r$ linear combinations of partial sums of $Mh_{T,t}$. Indeed we can prove the following proposition.

Proposition 2.1 *Under Assumption 2.2,*

$$d_t = B_\perp(F_\perp' B_\perp)^{-1} F_\perp' M \sum_{s=1}^{t} h_{T,s} + F(B'F)^{-1} \sum_{j=0}^{t-1} (I_r + B'F)^j B' M h_{T,t-j}. \tag{2.6}$$

Let $d_{t\perp}$ (d_{t*}) denotes the first (second) term of RHS of (2.6) and define

$$X_{D\perp}' = [d_{1\perp}, \ldots, d_{T\perp}]$$

and

$$X_{D*}' = [d_{1*}, \ldots, d_{T*}]. \tag{2.7}$$

Then, X_D can be expressed as

$$X_D = X_{D\perp} + X_{D*}, \tag{2.8}$$

where, because of $(SH_T)' = [h_{T,1}, \ldots, \sum_{s=1}^{T} h_{T,s}]$, $X_{D\perp}$ can be explicitly expressed as

$$X_{D\perp} = SH_T M' F_\perp (B'_\perp F_\perp)^{-1} B'_\perp. \tag{2.9}$$

Note that $X_{D\perp}$ is $O(T^{3/2})$, while X_{D*} is $O(T^{1/2})$ because $(I_r + B'F)$ is stable. It is also observed, from Definition 2.2(iv), that ΔX_{D*} is $O(1)$. In addition, we have

Lemma 2.2

$$X_{D*} = H_T M' B \sum_{j=0}^{\infty} (I_r + F'B)^j (F'B)^{-1} F' + O(1). \tag{2.10}$$

It is seen that B ($B_\perp$) performs the role of B ($B_\perp$) in Assumption 2.1, which has formulated the interrelated trends in terms of the orders as $T \to \infty$. Indeed we can see that (a) $X_D B$ is $O(T^{1/2})$ and (b) $X_D B_\perp \delta$ is not $o(T^{3/2})$ for any δ. (a) follows from $X_{D\perp} B = 0$, which implies that $X_D B = X_{D*} B$. (b) is proved as follows. In Assumption 2.2, rank$(M' F_\perp) = n - r$ implies that $M' F_\perp (B'_\perp F_\perp)^{-1} B'_\perp B_\perp$ has full column rank. Using (2.9) and Definition 2.2(iii), it is seen that $X_{D\perp} B_\perp$ has full column rank, while $X_{D*} B_\perp$ is dominated by $X_{D\perp} B_\perp$. In regard to (2.9), $SH_T M' F_\perp$ and $(B'_\perp F_\perp)^{-1} B'_\perp$ may be interpreted, respectively, as the common trends and as the allocation matrix which allocates the common trends among n variables. Alternatively, $SH_T M' F_\perp (B'_\perp F_\perp)^{-1}$ may be the common trends, and $B'_\perp$ the allocation matrix. In either case, the common trends are $n-r$ linear combinations of p elementary trend functions that are columns of the matrix SH_T. The relations among the trends of n variables are not exact because they allow residuals $X_D B = X_{D*} B$.

When $r = 0$, the matrices such as F, B, and $I_r + B'F$ do not exist, and $F_\perp$ and $B_\perp$ are both I_n. In this case, (2.6) is replaced by $\Delta d_t = M h_{T,t}$. Thus, we have

$$X_D = X_{D\perp} = SH_T M'. \tag{2.11}$$

We are now ready to return to Definition 2.2(ii). The selection of elementary trend functions, SH_T precedes all other studies required for our determination of $n - r$ from the time series data. It should be noted that this selection may imply some a priori condition introduced on the range in which $n - r$ is to be chosen. This is because the number of columns of SH_T, which is p, cannot be less than $n - r$ in order to have the rank of common trends, $SH_T M' F_\perp (B'_\perp F_\perp)^{-1}$, equal to $n - r$. Let *ctmax* denote the upper bound to the choice of $n-r$. If $p < n$ in the selection of SH_T, it means that we have introduced a priori the condition that $ctmax = p < n$. On the other hand, if $p > n$, it means nothing more than a trivial condition that $ctmax = n$. These points should be kept in mind in the selection of SH_T.[(1)]

2.3 Trend Functions

The theoretical analyses of this book will proceed without specifying concrete forms of the elementary functions, H_T, but it is useful to present here what we have in mind in implementing our parametric approach on the macroeconomic time series data. Let $0 < b_1 < \cdots < b_{p-1} < 1$, and $\boldsymbol{du}(b_j)$, $j = 1, \ldots, p-1$ be (2.4) with $b = b_j$. The concrete forms are

$$H_T = [\boldsymbol{\iota}, \boldsymbol{du}(b_1), \ldots, \boldsymbol{du}(b_{p-1})],$$
$$SH_T = [\boldsymbol{t}, \boldsymbol{dt}(b_1), \ldots, \boldsymbol{dt}(b_{p-1})], \tag{2.12}$$

and

$$\boldsymbol{dt}(b_j) = [0, \ldots, 0, 1, \ldots, T - [Tb_j]]'. \tag{2.13}$$

Thus, $p-1$ and $b_1, \ldots, b_{p-1}$ have to be properly selected prior to the implementation of the parametric approach. In fact, this requires investigation of the time series data of each variable to be included in X with regard to (i) the number of structural breaks in deterministic trends, and (ii) whether or not the break points are shared by the variables in X. The studies in Bai et al. (1998) and Yamada and Hatanaka (2002) are useful for this purpose, but the problem will not be discussed in this book. Columns of the common trends, $SH_TM'F_\perp$, with (2.12), represent piecewise linear functions of time with breaks located at $[Tb_1], \ldots, [Tb_{p-1}]$.

2.4 Co-trending and Co-breaking

The co-breaking in Hendry and Mizon (1998) and Clements and Hendry (1999) is the situation in a system of multivariate series such that each individual series contains a structural change but a linear combination of the series does not.(2) The structural change may be a step change or a slope change in the deterministic trends.

Co-breaking and co-trending can be compared in terms of the slope changes of trends if the elementary trend functions are given by (2.12) under Assumption 2.2. The co-breaking is concerned with a $n \times 1$ vector, γ, that annihilates asymptotically $[\boldsymbol{dt}(b_1), \ldots, \boldsymbol{dt}(b_{p-1})]$ from $T^{-3/2}X_D\gamma$. On the other hand the co-trending is concerned with a γ that annihilates asymptotically $T^{-3/2}X_D\gamma$ *entirely*. It is easy to show that the co-trending implies the co-breaking though the converse does not hold.

Let

$$P = M'F_\perp(B_\perp'F_\perp)^{-1}B_\perp'$$

so that $T^{-3/2}X_D\gamma \approx T^{-3/2}X_{D\perp}\gamma = T^{-3/2}SH_TP\gamma$ because of (2.9). $T^{-3/2}SH_T\,P\gamma = 0$ asymptotically if and only if $P\gamma = 0$. γ is a co-trending vector if and only if $P\gamma = 0$.

Therefore the co-trending rank is the dimension of the column null space of P, which is $n - \text{rank}(P)$.

As for the co-breaking, partition M' as

$$M' = \begin{bmatrix} m_1' \\ M_2' \end{bmatrix},$$

where m_1' is the first row of M'. Also write

$$P_2 = M_2' F_\perp (B_\perp' F_\perp)^{-1} B_\perp',$$

so that P_2 consists of the second, ..., the p-th row of P. (2.9) and (2.12) lead to

$$X_{D\perp} = \boldsymbol{t} m_1' F_\perp (B_\perp' F_\perp)^{-1} B_\perp' + [\boldsymbol{dt}(b_1), \ldots, \boldsymbol{dt}(b_{p-1})] P_2.$$

For a $n \times 1$ γ^* to annihilate $[\boldsymbol{dt}(b_1), \ldots, \boldsymbol{dt}(b_{p-1})]$ from $T^{-3/2} X_D \gamma^*$ asymptotically, it is necessary and sufficient to have $P_2 \gamma^* = 0$. γ^* is a co-breaking vector if and only if $P_2 \gamma^* = 0$. The number of linearly independent co-breaking vectors is the co-breaking rank. It is $n - \text{rank}(P_2)$.

Since each row of P_2 is a row of P, $P\gamma = 0$ implies $P_2 \gamma = 0$, i.e., a co-trending vector is necessarily a co-breaking vector. However the converse does not hold. The co-trending rank cannot exceed the co-breaking rank.

Co-breaking is useful to investigate the cause and nature of structural changes. Suppose that $n = 2$ and $p - 1 = 2$ so that SH_T involves $\boldsymbol{dt}(b_1)$ and $\boldsymbol{dt}(b_2)$. If the co-breaking rank is zero, the structural changes in the data of two variables may be regarded independent. If the co-breaking rank is 1, there must be a common factor of structural change which is propagated among the two variables. On the other hand, the co-trending is not directly concerned with the structural changes in deterministic trends. It is hoped to reveal a system of relations among the trends of different variables, and the structural changes are here a part of exogenous factors.

In Appendix C we shall explain how to determine the co-breaking rank from the data.

2.5 A Survey on the Direct and the Indirect Modelling of Trend

All of the time series models are built initially for a process with zero mean. Deterministic parts are introduced later as an extension of the initial model. For example, in a stationary AR(1), the model is initially

$$x_t = a x_{t-1} + \varepsilon_t,$$

and later the model is extended to

$$x_t = \mu + a x_{t-1} + \varepsilon_t.$$

It is notable here that $E(x_t)$ is not μ but $\mu/(1-a)$, and that it depends on a, which is a parameter of the stochastic part. As an another example, let us consider a simple model for the unit root test,

$$\Delta x_t = \alpha x_{t-1} + b_1 \Delta x_{t-1} + \varepsilon_t,$$

where $\alpha = 0$ for I(1) and $\alpha < 0$ for I(0). To introduce a linear deterministic trend, the model is extended to

$$\Delta x_t = \mu_0 + \mu_1 t + \alpha x_{t-1} + b_1 \Delta x_{t-1} + \varepsilon_t, \tag{2.14}$$

where $\alpha = 0$ and $\mu_1 = 0$ for I(1), while $\alpha < 0$ and μ_1 is unspecified for I(0). Let d_t be the deterministic part of x_t. The series of d_t is generated by the equation obtained from (2.14) by replacing x_t and x_{t-1} by d_t and d_{t-1} respectively and suppressing ε_t to zero, i.e.,

$$\Delta d_t = \mu_0 + \mu_1 t + \alpha d_{t-1} + b_1 \Delta d_{t-1}. \tag{2.15}$$

Then it can be seen that, if t is sufficiently large, the slope of the linear trend is $\mu_0/(1-b_1)$ for I(1), while it is $-\mu_1/\alpha$ for I(0), which depends upon α and b_1 in a complicated way. The modelling of deterministic trend that uses parameters of models of stochastic parts will be called indirect modelling of trend. Schmidt and Phillips (1992) criticised the modelling because of the difficulty of its interpretation, and developed a LM test of univariate unit root with direct modelling of trend. This was further followed in the point optimal invariance test of univariate unit root in Elliott et al. (1996).

In multivariate models, however, indirect modelling of trend is still dominating. The basic zero mean model was given in Johansen (1988), incorporating the cointegration. Then the deterministic trends have been introduced step by step. Johansen (1991 and 1994) introduced the linear trend. The latter is preferable because the vector of slopes in different variables is not constrained by the cointegration space. Johansen et al. (2000) added structural changes in levels and slopes of trends. In each case the model of d_t can be derived in the same way that (2.15) has been from (2.14). The parameterisation in the model is too complicated to determine the co-trending rank from the observations.(3) Indeed their method for the determination of cointegration rank assumes that the n variables contain n common deterministic trends, i.e., $r = 0$. See Appendix B.3.

3 Statistics from the Data Covariance Matrix

We shall utilise the information contained in the data covariance matrix to investigate the co-trending relations. Given an eigenvalue of the matrix, (i) the eigenvalue itself, (ii) the eigenvector associated with it, and (iii) the principal component associated with it form one set of statistics. Altogether n sets of statistics are available, and they are ordered in descending order in terms of the eigenvalues. In Section 3.1 below, the relations among the deterministic trends are classified into those that hold among the stochastic trends as well and those that do not hold among the stochastic trends. Let r_1 and r_2, respectively, represent the numbers of the former and the latter. By definition we have that $r = r_1 + r_2$. Section 3.2 will show that the first $n - r$ sets of statistics provide the information on the common deterministic trends. It will be shown in Section 3.3 that the next r_2 sets of statistics represent the relations that hold among the deterministic trends but do not hold among the stochastic trends. Section 3.4 will show that the last r_1 sets of statistics are related to the relations that hold among both the deterministic trends and the stochastic trends. Sections 3.5 and 3.6 will indicate how these results provide the bases for the testing procedures which will be given after Chapter 4. Section 3.6 contains an overview of the rest of this book.

All of the results in the present chapter will be derived in the non-parametric approach, which was given in Section 2.1. Correspondingly we introduce the following, general assumption on the stochastic part, s_t.

Assumption 3.1 *s_t in* (2.1) *is a n-variate non-degenerate ARIMA process with zero means, and its order of integration is at most 1.*

In the assumption above, the non-degeneracy means that $X_S\delta$ is not $o_p(T^{1/2})$ for any δ which is not equal to 0. It is secured by non-degeneracy of the innovation covariance matrix and by certain conditions on MA coefficients matrices. We do not introduce any structural changes into the parameters of the ARIMA process. As shown in Engle and Granger (1987), the cointegration matrix, β, which is a $n \times r_*$

full column rank matrix, is associated with the time series of s_t. The sequence of $\beta' s_t$ is I(0), and β represents the relations among the stochastic trends in X_S. Note that β above relates to the stochastic trends, while B in Assumption 2.1 has related to the deterministic trends.

3.1 Three-way Decomposition of the *n*-Dimensional Space

The n-dimensional space is decomposed first into csp($B_\perp$) and csp(B), and then csp(B) is orthogonally decomposed into that part that is in csp(β) and that part that is orthogonal to csp(β). Note that the initial division is between $B_\perp$ and B rather than between $\beta_\perp$ and β. This particular sequence of decomposition, while reflecting our basic strategy, conforms to our analyses of principal components of the data covariance matrix.

Given B and β, csp(B) ∩ csp(β) is obtained as follows. Let

$$r_1 = r + r_* - \text{rank}([B, \beta]).$$

The column null pace of $[B, \beta]$ has r_1 dimensions. Suppose that the space is spanned by $[G'_B, G'_\beta]'$, where G_B is $r \times r_1$ and G_β is $r_* \times r_1$. It can be shown that r_1 is the number of dimensions of csp(B) ∩ csp(β), implying that $r_1 \leq \min(r, r_*)$. Moreover we have

Lemma 3.1

$$\text{csp}(B) \cap \text{csp}(\beta) = \text{csp}(BG_B) = \text{csp}(\beta G_\beta).$$

Let $B_1 = BG_B$. Then B_1 represents the relations which hold not only among the deterministic trends but also among the stochastic trends. $X_D B_1$ is $O(T^{1/2})$. $X_S B_1$ is I(0) with zero mean and $O_p(T^{1/2})$. Since $B' BG_B$ is $r \times r_1$ with rank r_1, there exists D' such that $D' B' BG_B = 0$, and D' is $(r - r_1) \times r$ with rank $r - r_1$. Write $B_2 = BD$. Then csp(B_2) ⊂ csp(B), csp(B_2) ⊥ csp(B_1), and csp(B) = csp($[B_1, B_2]$). B_2 represents some relations among deterministic trends, but does not represent any relations among stochastic trends. $X_D B_2$ is $O(T^{1/2})$. $X_S B_2$ is I(1) with zero mean, *not cointegrated*, and $O_p(T)$. We shall write

$$r_2 = r - r_1.$$

Finally $B_\perp$ is crucial to the formation of the common deterministic trends, $X_D B_\perp$. $X_S B_\perp$ may contain elements of I(1) and I(0) in the sense that $X_S B_\perp \delta$ is I(1) for some δ but I(0) for some other δ. However, an explicit decomposition of csp($B_\perp$) into the part that is and the part that is not in csp(β) will not be needed in our analyses.

We have constructed $B_\perp$, B_2, and B_1. They are $n \times (n-r)$, $n \times r_2$, and $n \times r_1$, respectively, and mutually orthogonal. We assume that

$$\boldsymbol{B} = [B_\perp, B_2, B_1]$$

is a $n \times n$ orthogonal matrix. It will simplify presentation of our results. It will not restrain their validity, because Assumption 2.1 specifies properties of csp(B) and csp($B_\perp$) equally applicable to every particular representation of these spaces. Incidentally, the orthogonality of $\boldsymbol{B}$ still leaves representations of $B_\perp$, B_2, and B_1 non-unique because, for example, $B_\perp$ may be replaced by $B_\perp \Gamma$, where Γ is an arbitrary orthogonal matrix.

The data covariance matrix is defined as

$$T^{-3}X'(I - \boldsymbol{P}(\iota))X. \tag{3.1}$$

The denominator is T^3 because trends are involved in X. Let $\hat{\lambda}_1 > \hat{\lambda}_2 > \cdots > \hat{\lambda}_n$ be the eigenvalues of (3.1). The eigenvector that corresponds to $\hat{\lambda}_i$ is denoted by $\hat{\xi}_i$. The corresponding principal component is $(I - \boldsymbol{P}(\iota))X\hat{\xi}_i$. We consider that $\hat{\lambda}_i$, $\hat{\xi}_i$, and $(I-\boldsymbol{P}(\iota))X\hat{\xi}_i$ form one set of statistics, the i-th set. Altogether we have n sets. The rest of the present chapter analyses them, assuming that r, r_2, and r_1 are given. It will be shown that the n sets of statistics are classified into 3 groups. The first group consists of the sets that correspond to $\hat{\lambda}_1, \ldots, \hat{\lambda}_{n-r}$. The first group is never null because we have excluded $r = n$ in Assumption 2.1. The second group of sets corresponds to $\hat{\lambda}_{n-r+1}, \ldots, \hat{\lambda}_{n-r_1}$. This group is null if $r_2 = 0$. The third group corresponds to $\hat{\lambda}_{n-r_1+1}, \ldots, \hat{\lambda}_n$. This group is null if $r_1 = 0$. It will be seen that the first, the second, and the third groups are closely related to $B_\perp$, B_2, and B_1, respectively. In order to have memorisable names we shall call the first, the second, and the third groups (of sets of statistics), respectively, Group $\perp$ (to be pronounced 'perp'), Group 2, and Group 1. Assumptions 2.1 and 3.1 are basic in the following development, but additional assumptions will be introduced as we go along. In Chapter 3 X, X_D, and X_S will mean *the demeaned* X, X_D, *and* X_S, respectively.

3.2 Group ⊥

Assumption 3.2 *We assume that (i)* $G = \lim_{T\to\infty} T^{-3}X_D'X_D$ *exists and (ii)*

$$T^{-3}X_D'X_D - G$$

is $O(T^{-1/2})$.

Partly because $GB_2 = 0$ and $GB_1 = 0$ by Assumption 2.1 and partly because $\boldsymbol{B}$ is orthogonal, the positive eigenvalues of G are the eigenvalues of the $(n-r) \times (n-r)$ nonsingular matrix,

$$G_{\perp\perp} = B'_{\perp} G B_{\perp}.$$

We denote the eigenvalues by $\lambda_1, \cdots, \lambda_{n-r}$ in descending order. The eigenvectors of G associated with $\lambda_1, \ldots, \lambda_{n-r}$ are denoted by $\xi_{D,1}, \ldots, \xi_{D,n-r}$, each of which is $n \times 1$, and the eigenvectors of $G_{\perp\perp}$ by $\eta_{\perp,1}, \ldots \eta_{\perp,n-r}$, each of which is $(n-r) \times 1$. All the eigenvectors are ortho-normalised. It is easy to show that $\xi_{D,i} = B_{\perp}\eta_{\perp,i}$ for $i = 1, \ldots, n-r$.(4) However, note that $\xi_{D,i}$ is determined by G without using $B_{\perp}$. Indeed $B_{\perp}\eta_{\perp,i}$ is invariant through replacement of $B_{\perp}$ by $B_{\perp}\Gamma$, where Γ is an arbitrary orthogonal matrix. On the other hand, $\hat{\lambda}_i$ and $\hat{\xi}_i$ refer to the data covariance matrix, (3.1).

Proposition 3.1 *From Assumptions 2.1, 3.1, and 3.2 and from the construction of $B_{\perp}$, B_2, and B_1, we obtain the following results:*

(i) $[\hat{\lambda}_1, \ldots, \hat{\lambda}_{n-r}]$ *converges in probability to* $[\lambda_1, \ldots, \lambda_{n-r}]$.
(ii) $[\hat{\xi}_1, \ldots, \hat{\xi}_{n-r}]$ *converges in probability to* $[\xi_{D,1}, \ldots, \xi_{D,n-r}]$.
(iii) When $\boldsymbol{B}$ is used as the system of coordinates so that $[\hat{\xi}_1, \ldots, \hat{\xi}_{n-r}] = B_{\perp}\Gamma_{\perp\perp} + B_2\Gamma_{2\perp} + B_1\Gamma_{1\perp}$, *then we have that*

$$\Gamma_{\perp\perp} = [\eta_{\perp,1}, \ldots, \eta_{\perp,n-r}] + O_p(T^{-1/2}) \tag{3.2}$$

and that both $\Gamma_{2\perp}$ and $\Gamma_{1\perp}$ are $O_p(T^{-1/2})$.
(iv) $X[\hat{\xi}_1, \ldots, \hat{\xi}_{n-r}]$ *is $O_p(T^{3/2})$ such that*

$$T^{-3/2}X[\hat{\xi}_1, \ldots, \hat{\xi}_{n-r}] = T^{-3/2}X_D B_{\perp}[\eta_{\perp,1}, \ldots, \eta_{\perp,n-r}] + O_p(T^{-1/2}). \tag{3.3}$$

In Group $\perp$, the eigenvalues and eigenvectors of the data covariance matrix converge, respectively, to the positive eigenvalues and the associated eigenvectors of G. (ii) is implied in (iii), but shown separately for its importance. (ii) and (iii) may be interpreted to mean that $\mathrm{csp}([\hat{\xi}_1, \ldots, \hat{\xi}_{n-r}])$ converges to $\mathrm{csp}(B_{\perp})$. (iv) means that the largest $n-r$ principal components converge to the common trends. Here, $[\eta_{\perp,1}, \ldots, \eta_{\perp,n-r}]$ is nonstochastic unlike the corresponding situations in Group 2 and Group 1.

3.3 Group 2

By construction, $X_S B_2$ is I(1) with zero mean, and not cointegrated. Construct

$$W_T^{(2)} = [T^{-3/2}X_D B_{\perp}, T^{-1}X_S B_2]'[T^{-3/2}X_D B_{\perp}, T^{-1}X_S B_2].$$

Assumption 3.3 *We assume that (i) $W_T^{(2)}$ weakly converges to*

$$W^{(2)} = \begin{bmatrix} G_{\perp\perp} & W_{\perp 2} \\ W_{2\perp} & W_{22} \end{bmatrix}, \tag{3.4}$$

and (ii) $W_T^{(2)} - W^{(2)}$ is $O_p(T^{-1/2})$.[5]

Note that both W_{22} and $W_{2\perp}$ are stochastic while $G_{\perp\perp}$ is nonstochastic. Define

$$U_{22} = W_{22} - W_{2\perp} G_{\perp\perp}^{-1} W_{2\perp}', \tag{3.5}$$

which is what

$$T^{-2} B_2' X_S' (I - P(X_D B_\perp)) X_S B_2 \tag{3.6}$$

weakly converges to. Since $W^{(2)}$ is a.s. positive definite, so is U_{22}. Let $\lambda_i(U_{22})$, $i = 1, \ldots, r_2$, be the i-th eigenvalue of U_{22} arranged in descending order, and let $\eta_{2,i}$, $i = 1, \ldots, r_2$, be the corresponding ortho-normalised eigenvectors. It is easy to see that the positive eigenvalues of $B_2 U_{22} B_2'$ are $\lambda_1(U_{22}), \ldots, \lambda_{r_2}(U_{22})$, and also that the corresponding eigenvectors are $B_2\eta_{2,1}, \ldots, B_2\eta_{2,r_2}$. It is seen from (3.5) and (3.6) that $B_2 U_{22} B_2'$ remains unchanged when B_2 is replaced by $B_2\Gamma$, where Γ is an arbitrary $r_2 \times r_2$ orthogonal matrix. Therefore $\lambda_i(U_{22})$ and $B_2\eta_{2,i}$, $i = 1, \ldots, r_2$ are uniquely determined in spite of the non-uniqueness of B_2 mentioned earlier. When $r_2 = 1$, $\eta_{2,i}$ is reduced to the scalar constant, 1.

Proposition 3.2 *Suppose that $r_2 > 0$. From Assumptions 2.1, 3.1, and 3.3 and from the construction of $B_\perp$, B_2, and B_1, we obtain the following results:*

(i) $T[\hat{\lambda}_{n-r+1}, \ldots, \hat{\lambda}_{n-r_1}]$ *weakly converges to* $[\lambda_1(U_{22}), \ldots, \lambda_{r_2}(U_{22})]$.
(ii) $[\hat{\xi}_{n-r+1}, \ldots, \hat{\xi}_{n-r_1}]$ *weakly converges to* $B_2[\eta_{2,1}, \ldots, \eta_{2,r_2}]$.
*(iii) When **B** is used as the system of coordinates so that*

$$[\hat{\xi}_{n-r+1}, \ldots, \hat{\xi}_{n-r_1}] = B_\perp \Gamma_{\perp 2} + B_2 \Gamma_{22} + B_1 \Gamma_{12},$$

then we have $\Gamma_{\perp 2}$ is $O_p(T^{-1/2})$. More precisely,

$$\Gamma_{\perp 2} = -T^{-1/2} G_{\perp\perp}^{-1} W_{2\perp}' [\eta_{2,1}, \ldots, \eta_{2,r_2}] + O_p(T^{-1}). \tag{3.7}$$

We also have that Γ_{12} is $O_p(T^{-1/2})$ and

$$\Gamma_{22} = [\eta_{2,1}, \ldots, \eta_{2,r_2}] + O_p(T^{-1/2}). \tag{3.8}$$

(iv) $X[\hat{\xi}_{n-r+1},\ldots,\hat{\xi}_{n-r_1+1}]$ *is* $O_p(T)$ *such that*

$$T^{-1}X[\hat{\xi}_{n-r+1},\ldots,\hat{\xi}_{n-r_1}] = T^{-1}(I - P(X_D B_\perp))X_S B_2[\eta_{2,1},\ldots,\eta_{2,r_2}] + O_p(T^{-1/2}). \quad (3.9)$$

In Group 2 the eigenvalues of the data covariance matrix are $O_p(T^{-1})$. T times the eigenvalues remain random variables as $T \to \infty$, which converge to the positive eigenvalues of $B_2 U_{22} B_2'$. When $r_2 \geq 2$ the eigenvectors of the data covariance matrix also remain stochastic, which converge to the eigenvectors of $B_2 U_{22} B_2'$ associated with its positive eigenvalues. When $r_2 = 1$, $\eta_{2,i}$ is the scalar constant, 1, and the eigenvector of the data covariance matrix converges in probability to the vector, B_2. The principal components in Group 2 are related to $X_S B_2$, but more accurately they belong to the space obtained by projecting $X_S B_2$ on the orthogonal complement of $X_D B_\perp$ (common trends). Moreover, when $r_2 \geq 2$, what are projected are not $X_S B_2$ but their combinations with random coefficients, $\eta_{2,i}$.

3.4 Group 1

Construct

$$W_T^{(1)} = [T^{-3/2}X_D B_\perp, T^{-1}X_S B_2, T^{-1/2}X_D B_1]'[T^{-3/2}X_D B_\perp, T^{-1}X_S B_2, T^{-1/2}X_D B_1].$$

Assumption 3.4 *We assume that (i)* $W_T^{(1)}$ *weakly converges to*

$$W^{(1)} = \begin{bmatrix} G_{\perp\perp} & W_{\perp 2} & G_{\perp 1} \\ W_{2\perp} & W_{22} & W_{21} \\ G_{1\perp} & W_{12} & G_{11} \end{bmatrix} \quad (3.10)$$

and (ii) $W_T^{(1)} - W^{(1)}$ *is* $O_p(T^{-1/2})$.

Note that G_{11}, $G_{1\perp}$, and $G_{\perp\perp}$ are nonstochastic, while W_{12}, W_{22}, and $W_{2\perp}$ are stochastic. In addition, $X_S B_1$ is I(0) with zero mean. Define

$$U_{11} = F_{11} + G_{11} - [G_{1\perp}, W_{12}] \begin{bmatrix} G_{\perp\perp} & W_{\perp 2} \\ W_{2\perp} & W_{22} \end{bmatrix}^{-1} \begin{bmatrix} G_{1\perp}' \\ W_{12}' \end{bmatrix}, \quad (3.11)$$

where $F_{11} = \text{plim}_{T\to\infty} T^{-1}B_1'X_S'X_S B_1$. Then, we can see that

$$T^{-1}B_1'X(I - P([X_D B_\perp, X_S B_2]))X B_1 \xrightarrow{w} U_{11}. \quad (3.12)$$

This follows partly from $F_{11} + G_{11} = \mathrm{plim}_{T\to\infty} T^{-1}B_1'X'XB_1$ and partly from

$$T^{-1}B_1'X'P([X_DB_\perp, X_SB_2])XB_1 = T^{-1}B_1'X_D'P([X_DB_\perp, X_SB_2])X_DB_1 + O_p(T^{-1/2})$$
$$\xrightarrow{w} \text{the third term on the RHS of (3.11).}$$

U_{11} is a.s. positive definite. Let $\lambda_1(U_{11}), \ldots, \lambda_{r_1}(U_{11})$ be the eigenvalues of matrix U_{11} in descending order, and let $\eta_{1,1}, \ldots, \eta_{1,r_1}$ be the corresponding orthonormalised eigenvectors. The positive eigenvalues of the $n \times n$ matrix $B_1U_{11}B_1'$ are $\lambda_1(U_{11}), \ldots, \lambda_{r_1}(U_{11})$, and the corresponding eigenvectors are $B_1\eta_{1,1}, \ldots, B_1\eta_{1,r_1}$. When $r_1 = 1, \eta_{1,i}$ is reduced to 1.

Proposition 3.3 *Suppose that $r_1 > 0$. From Assumptions 2.1, 3.1, and 3.4 and from the construction of $B_\perp$, B_2, and B_1, we have the following results:*

(i) $T^2[\hat{\lambda}_{n-r_1+1}, \ldots, \hat{\lambda}_n]$ *weakly converges to* $[\lambda_1(U_{11}), \ldots, \lambda_{r_1}(U_{11})]$.
(ii) $[\hat{\xi}_{n-r_1+1}, \ldots, \hat{\xi}_n]$ *weakly converges to* $B_1[\eta_{1,1}, \ldots, \eta_{1,r_1}]$.
(iii) *When* $\boldsymbol{B}$ *is used as the coordinate system so that*

$$[\hat{\xi}_{n-r_1+1}, \ldots, \hat{\xi}_n] = B_\perp\Gamma_{\perp 1} + B_2\Gamma_{21} + B_1\Gamma_{11},$$

we have that $\Gamma_{11} = [\eta_{1,1}, \ldots, \eta_{1,r_1}] + O_p(T^{-1/2})$ *and that* Γ_{21} *and* $\Gamma_{\perp 1}$ *are respectively* $O_p(T^{-1/2})$ *and* $O_p(T^{-1})$. *In fact, denoting*

$$\begin{bmatrix} G_{\perp\perp} & W_{\perp 2} \\ W_{2\perp} & W_{22} \end{bmatrix}^{-1} = \begin{bmatrix} A_\perp \\ A_2 \end{bmatrix}, \tag{3.13}$$

we have

$$\Gamma_{\perp 1} = -T^{-1}A_\perp[G_{1\perp}, W_{12}]'[\eta_{1,1}, \ldots, \eta_{1,r_1}] + O_p(T^{-3/2}),$$

and

$$\Gamma_{21} = -T^{-1/2}A_2[G_{1\perp}, W_{12}]'[\eta_{1,1}, \ldots, \eta_{1,r_1}] + O_p(T^{-1}).$$

(iv) $X[\hat{\xi}_{n-r_1+1}, \ldots, \hat{\xi}_n]$ *is* $O_p(T^{1/2})$ *such that*

$$T^{-1/2}X[\hat{\xi}_{n-r_1+1}, \ldots, \hat{\xi}_n] = T^{-1/2}((I - P(X_DB_\perp)) - P((I - P(X_DB_\perp))X_SB_2))XB_1[\eta_{1,1}, \ldots, \eta_{1,r_1}] + O_p(T^{-1/2}). \tag{3.14}$$

In Group 1, T^2 times the eigenvalues of the data covariance matrix converge to the positive eigenvalues of stochastic $B_1U_{11}B_1'$. When $r_1 \geq 2$, the eigenvectors of the data covariance matrix converge to the associated eigenvectors of $B_1U_{11}B_1'$. When

$r_1 = 1$, the eigenvector converges to B_1. Regarding the expressions of the principal components, notice that the projections on $[X_D B_\perp, X_S B_2]$ are subtracted from X. All the above expressions have been given for the case where $r_2 > 0$, but the only modification that is required when $r_2 = 0$, while $r_1 > 0$, is to delete the matrices associated with Group 2.

3.5 An Approximation of $P(X)$

It is known that $\boldsymbol{P}(X)$ is exactly the sum of $\boldsymbol{P}(X\hat{\xi}_i)$, $i = 1, \ldots, n$. We shall later need a more crude decomposition of csp(X). We define two projection matrices being approximately equal. Let both A and B be possibly stochastic, $T \times k$, matrices with a given k. Let x be a non-stochastic, $T \times 1$, column vector and arbitrary except for that $\| x \| = 1$, and suppose that neither $\boldsymbol{P}(A)x$ nor $\boldsymbol{P}(B)x$ is $o_p(1)$ for any x as $T \to \infty$. If $(\boldsymbol{P}(A) - \boldsymbol{P}(B))x$ is nevertheless $O_p(T^{-1/2})$ for any x, then we shall write $\boldsymbol{P}(A) \approx \boldsymbol{P}(B)$.

Proposition 3.4 *Under Assumptions 2.1 and 3.1,*

$$\boldsymbol{P}(X) \approx \boldsymbol{P}(X_D B_\perp) + \boldsymbol{P}((I - \boldsymbol{P}(X_D B_\perp))X_S B_2) + \boldsymbol{P}((I - \boldsymbol{P}(X_D B_\perp)) - \boldsymbol{P}((I - \boldsymbol{P}(X_D B_\perp))X_S B_2)XB_1). \quad (3.15)$$

Combining this proposition with (iv) of each of Propositions 3.1, 3.2, and 3.3, we see the roles that the principal components can play. Proposition 3.4 will also play an important role in Chapter 6.

3.6 Plan for the Rest of the Book

Among r (or $n - r$), r_2, and r_1, the determination of r is most useful for empirical studies of macroeconomic times series. However, the inference on B is also useful, and it would require the determination of r_2 and r_1 prior to the inference. We shall attempt to determine r, r_2, and r_1 jointly. Given r, r_2, and r_1, the statistics of the data covariance matrix have been classified into three groups in regard to the association with (i) $\hat{\lambda}_1 > \cdots > \hat{\lambda}_{n-r}$ (altogether $n-r$ roots), (ii) $\hat{\lambda}_{n-r+1} > \cdots > \hat{\lambda}_{n-r_1}$ (altogether r_2 roots), and (iii) $\hat{\lambda}_{n-r_1+1} > \cdots > \hat{\lambda}_n$ (altogether r_1 roots). Let us focus our attention on the principal components. Those in Group $\perp$ have trends that are $O(T^{3/2})$ as shown in (3.3), while their stochastic parts may be either I(1) or I(0). Those in Group 2 have no trends as shown in (3.9), and their stochastic parts are essentially I(1), though projections on trends are subtracted. Those in Group 1 also have no trends as shown in (3.14), but their stochastic parts are essentially I(0). In the following, we use the unit root test and trend test to classify the principal components into the three groups. When the three groups are discerned, the numbers of constituents of the three groups, i.e., $n-r$, r_2, and r_1 are determined. The unit root test and the trend test are feasible only when the parametric approach is adopted to represent the interrelated deterministic trends by elementary trend functions.

Let us give an overview of the chapters in the rest of the book. Our decision rule is presented in Chapter 7. Before Chapter 7, the properties of various statistics will be investigated under the assumption that $n-r$, r_2, and r_1 are known. Chapter 4 describes minor, nonstandard terms contained in the principal components in all three groups. Chapter 5 will show that the standard unit root test and its multivariate extension achieve their purpose in spite of these nonstandard terms. Chapter 6 will discuss trend tests. In this chapter, the nonstandard terms completely hamper the standard approaches such as F tests in the presence of both I(0) and I(1) stochastic terms. In the case of I(0), the presence and absence of trends can be discriminated by an elementary method. In the case of I(1), we shall propose an ad hoc method, but its limiting distribution depends on a unknown matrix parameter. As it is replaced by a consistent estimate in implementing the test, the critical value is data-dependent. Even though $n-r$, r_2, and r_1 are assumed to be known in Chapters 5 and 6, each chapter will contain analyses of how the mistaken $n-r$, r_2, and r_1 affect results of the unit root and the trend tests. The analyses will be used in developing the decision rule to determine $n-r$, r_2, and r_1 in Chapter 7. Simulation studies will be shown in Chapter 8, including investigation of the data-dependent critical value.

Incidentally, the eigenvalues of the data covariance matrix are also useful because $T[\hat{\lambda}_{n-r+1}, \ldots, \hat{\lambda}_n]$ is $O_p(1)$ while $T\hat{\lambda}_{n-r}$ diverges to ∞ as $T \to \infty$. Hatanaka (2000) used the eigenvalues to determine r in a model of co-trending which is different from the present one. Since then the method has been adapted to the present model, but it will not be presented in this book.(6) The reasons are that it implicitly assumes $r_2 \neq 0$ (though not invalid when $r_2 = 0$), and that it does not separate r_2 and r_1.

4 Principal Components

The results in the previous chapter have been derived by the non-parametric approach. Hereafter, the co-trending will be modelled by the parametric approach using Assumption 2.2 with some elementary trend functions. The purpose is to make the DGP of principal components sufficiently specific so that statistical tests can be applied to the principal components. Propositions 3.1 through 3.3 of the previous chapter have been derived from Assumptions 2.1, 3.1, 3.2, 3.3, and 3.4 based on the non-parametric approach. In translating these results onto the parametric approach, Assumptions 2.1, 3.2, 3.3, and 3.4 are derived from Assumption 2.2 and Definition 2.2. Definition 2.2 specifies the conditions to be met by the elementary trend functions, and it will be considered as a part of Assumption 2.2. Thus our basic assumptions in the parametric approach are Assumptions 2.2 and 3.1.

In the previous chapter, the demeaned X, X_D, and X_S were abbreviated as X, X_D, and X_S. This abbreviation is not made in the present chapter. $\hat{\xi}_i$ below is the eigenvector of (3.1) as it was in the previous chapter. The principal component was written $X\hat{\xi}_i$ in the previous chapter, but it is really $(I - P(\iota))X\hat{\xi}_i$. G is $\lim_{T\to\infty} T^{-3}X_D'(I - P(\iota))X_D$, and $\eta_{\perp,i}$ below is the eigenvector of $B_\perp' G B_\perp$. U_{22} is what

$$T^{-2}B_2'X_S'((I - P(\iota)) - P((I - P(\iota))X_D B_\perp))X_S B_2$$

weakly converges to, and $\eta_{2,i}$ is its eigenvector. Likewise on U_{11}. We shall omit the subscript, T, in H_T and SH_T. In connection with (2.9), let us set $Q \equiv M'F_\perp(B_\perp'F_\perp)^{-1}$. Since $B_\perp'B_\perp = I_{n-r}$,

$$X_{D\perp} = SHQB_\perp', \ X_{D\perp}B_\perp = SHQ, \text{ and } X_{D\perp}B = 0. \tag{4.1}$$

In the rest of the book, Q is the coefficient matrix to form the common deterministic trends from SH, and $B_\perp'$ is the allocation matrix. Neither Q nor $B_\perp'$ is unique in the representation of the interrelated trends, but $QB_\perp'$ is. In connection with (2.10), let us set

$$K \equiv M'B \sum_{j=0}^{\infty} (I + F'B)^j (F'B)^{-1} F'$$

so that

$$X_{D*} = HK + O(1). \tag{4.2}$$

Regarding X_D in (2.8), $X_D B = X_{D*} B = HKB + O(1)$ and $X_D B_\perp = SHQ + HKB_\perp + O(1)$. $SHQ\delta$ is $O(T^{3/2})$, not $o(T^{3/2})$, for any non-zero δ. H is $O(T^{1/2})$. ΔX_{D*} is $O(1)$ as noted in Chapter 2.

The purpose of the present chapter is to present explicit expressions of the DGP of principal components in Group $\perp$, Group 2, and Group 1. It will be seen that the principal components are not standard time series that have been postulated in the unit root test. We shall examine the applicability of the test in the next chapter. It will be found there that the *null* model of the test, which is $I(1)$, should be examined closely to ensure the validity of the limit distribution of the test statistic. In particular, in dealing with the differenced series, we shall have to examine even the terms in $O_p(1)$ in Group 2 of principal components and also in Group $\perp$ where $B_\perp \eta_{\perp,i}$ is not a cointegration vector. This explains why complicated expressions appear in the following propositions. On the other hand, the unit root test will be found fairly robust to deviations from the standard specifications of the *alternative* models, which are I(0).

4.1 Group $\perp$, $i = 1, \ldots, n - r$

$\eta_{\perp,i}$ is the eigenvector of $G_{\perp\perp} = \lim_{T\to\infty} T^{-3} Q'H'S'(I - \boldsymbol{P}(\iota))SHQ$.

Proposition 4.1 *Suppose that Assumptions 2.2 and 3.1 hold. Then, $(I - \boldsymbol{P}(\iota))X\hat{\xi}_i$ for $i = 1, \ldots, n - r$ can be represented as follows.*

(i) *If $B_\perp \eta_{\perp,i}$ is not a cointegration vector, it is expressed as*

$$(I - \boldsymbol{P}(\iota))X\hat{\xi}_i = (I - \boldsymbol{P}(\iota))[SHQ\eta_{\perp,i} + X_S B_\perp \eta_{\perp,i} + SHQ\delta_{1i}] + O_p(T^{1/2}), \tag{4.3}$$

where δ_{1i} is $O_p(T^{-1/2})$, and it follows that

$$\Delta X\hat{\xi}_i = HQ\eta_{\perp,i} + \Delta X_S B_\perp \eta_{\perp,i} + \zeta_i + O_p(T^{-1/2}), \tag{4.4}$$

where

$$\zeta_i = \Delta X_S B_1 \delta_{2i} + \Delta X_S B_2 \delta_{3i} + \Delta X_S B_\perp \delta_{4i} + HQ\delta_{5i} + \Delta X_{D*} B_\perp \eta_{\perp,i}, \tag{4.5}$$

δ_{2i}, δ_{3i}, δ_{4i}, and δ_{5i} are $O_p(T^{-1/2})$ so that ζ_i is $O_p(1)$. H in (4.5) is not demeaned.

(ii) *If $B_{\perp}\eta_{\perp,i}$ is a cointegration vector, it is expressed as*

$$(I - P(\iota))X\hat{\xi}_i = (I - P(\iota))[SHQ\eta_{\perp,i} + SHQ\delta_{1i} + HKB_{\perp i} + X_S B_{\perp}\eta_{\perp,i} + X_S B_{\perp}\delta_{2i}] + O_p(1), \quad (4.6)$$

where both δ_{1i} and δ_{2i} are $O_p(T^{-1/2})$ and $B_{\perp i}$ is the i-th column of $B_{\perp}$, and it follows that

$$\Delta X\hat{\xi}_i = HQ\eta_{\perp,i} + \Delta X_S B_{\perp}\eta_{\perp,i} + O_p(1). \quad (4.7)$$

Proposition 4.1 is obtained by (i) substituting the result on $\hat{\xi}_i$ in Proposition 3.1(iii) into $(I - P(\iota))X\hat{\xi}_i$, and (ii) rewriting the expressions in terms of the parametric approach with (2.8), (4.1), and (4.2). In investigating the orders of various terms involved we note that $X_S B_{\perp}\eta_{\perp,i}$ is I(1) if $B_{\perp}\eta_{\perp,i}$ is not in csp(β), and I(0) if $B_{\perp}\eta_{\perp,i}$ is in csp(β).

4.2 Group 2, $i = n - r + 1, \ldots, n - r_1, r_2 > 0$

$\eta_{2,i}$ has been the eigenvector of a random matrix, U_{22}.

Proposition 4.2 *Suppose that Assumptions 2.2 and 3.1 hold. For $i = n-r+1, \ldots, n-r_1$, $(I - P(\iota))X\hat{\xi}_i$ can be represented as*

$$(I - P(\iota))X\hat{\xi}_i = (I - P([\iota, SHQ]))X_S B_2\eta_{2,i} + O_p(T^{1/2}), \quad (4.8)$$

and it follows that

$$\Delta X\hat{\xi}_i = \Delta X_S B_2\eta_{2,i} + \zeta_i + O_p(T^{-1/2}), \quad (4.9)$$

where ζ_i is in the same form as (4.5).

Notice that $\eta_{2,i}$ in (4.8) and (4.9) is the scalar, 1, when $r_2 = 1$.

4.3 Group 1, $i = n - r_1 + 1, \ldots, n, r_1 > 0$

$\eta_{1,i}$ has been the eigenvector of a random matrix, U_{11}.

Proposition 4.3 *Suppose that Assumptions 2.2 and 3.1 hold. For $i = n-r_1+1, \ldots, n$, $(I - P(\iota))X\hat{\xi}_i$ can be represented as*

$$(I - P(\iota))X\hat{\xi}_i = (I - P(\iota))X_S B_1\eta_{1,i} + (I - P([\iota, X_S B_2, SHQ]))HKB_1\eta_{1,i} + O_p(1), \quad (4.10)$$

and it follows that

$$\Delta X\hat{\xi}_i = \Delta X_S B_1\eta_{1,i} + O_p(1), \quad (4.11)$$

where $\eta_{1,i}$ in (4.10) *and* (4.11) *is the scalar, 1, when $r_1 = 1$.*

5 Unit Root Tests

We shall prove that the minor, nonstandard terms in principal components do not affect the applicability of the unit root tests. Both the univariate and the multivariate unit root tests are considered. The univariate unit root test, which is the well known method in Perron (1989), is expected to be applied to each individual principal component in Group $\perp$, one principal component in Group 2 when $r_2 = 1$, and each individual component in Group 1. The test will be described in Section 5.1. It will be followed in Sections 5.2 and 5.3 by our proofs of its applicability to the principal components in Group $\perp$, and in Section 5.4 by its applicability to Group 2 and Group 1. The multivariate unit root test is a test for zero cointegration rank in Johansen et al. (2000). It is expected to be applied to the entire set of principal components in Group 2 when $r_2 \geq 2$. The method will be described in Section 5.5, and our proof of its applicability to Group 2 will be given in Section 5.6. So far we have assumed that the correct division among Groups $\perp$, 2, and 1 is known, and that the division is used to assign the correct unit root tests to the principal components. In Section 5.7, we shall analyse the effects that incorrect divisions among the three Groups would bring about.

As for the stochastic part, Assumption 3.1 has been introduced in Chapter 3. Here it is reinforced by

Assumption 5.1 *Let γ be a non-stochastic $n \times 1$ vector. (i) If $X_S\gamma$ is I(0), it is a stationary ARMA process (with zero mean) of which the MA is invertible. (ii) If $X_S\gamma$ is I(1), $\Delta X_S\gamma$ is a stationary ARMA (with zero mean) of which the MA is invertible.*

In general, if the series of $x_t = [x_{1t}, \ldots, x_{nt}]'$ is a stationary vector AR, its single element, say, the series of x_{1t} can be regarded as a stationary ARMA. However, its MA part may not be invertible. Assumptions 3.1 and 5.1 combined are a little stronger than, for example, the model in Johansen (1988).

5.1 Univariate Unit Root Test

A standard unit root test applied to a univariate series, $x_t, t = 1, \ldots, T$, with lag order, k, is the following procedure in the case where the deterministic components, H and SH, are involved. This test has been developed in Dickey and Fuller (1979) and Perron (1989). Let k be an integer that may be 0, and construct $x = [x_{k+2}, \ldots, x_T]'$, $x_{-1} = [x_{k+1}, \ldots, x_{T-1}]'$, and $\Delta x_{-i} = [\Delta x_{k-i+2}, \ldots, \Delta x_{T-i}]'$ for $i = 0, \ldots k$. Δx_0 will be written as Δx. A set of elementary functions, H, $T \times p$ is given, and its t-th row is h_t'. We shall write $SH = [\sum_{s=1}^{k+2} h_s, \ldots, \sum_{s=1}^{T} h_s]'$. Construct (i) for $k \geq 1$,

$$Z = [H, SH, x_{-1}, \Delta x_{-1}, \ldots, \Delta x_{-k}], \tag{5.1}$$

$$Z_0 = [H, \Delta x_{-1}, \ldots, \Delta x_{-k}], \tag{5.2}$$

and (ii) for $k = 0$, $Z = [H, SH, x_{-1}]$ and $Z_0 = H$. With these matrices, the unit root test statistic with lag order, k, is written as

$$UURT \equiv [(T - 2k - 2p - 2)^{-1}\Delta x'(I - \boldsymbol{P}(Z))\Delta x]^{-1} \\ \times [(p + 1)^{-1}\Delta x'(\boldsymbol{P}(Z) - \boldsymbol{P}(Z_0))\Delta x]. \tag{5.3}$$

$UURT$ is the abbreviation of univariate unit root test. $(T - 2k - 2p - 2)^{-1}$ and $(p + 1)^{-1}$ reflect the view that regards (5.3) as the F statistic to test for the zero coefficient vector on $[SH, x_{-1}]$.(7) For the time being none of H, SH, x, and Δx is demeaned.

The distribution to be fitted to this statistic is constructed as follows. Let τ be a real scalar variable on $[0, 1]$, and let $B(\tau)$ be a scalar, standard Brownian motion process. We write continuous time representations of H and SH as $h(\tau)$ and $g(\tau)$ ($p \times 1$ each), respectively. Let g_t' denote the t-th row of SH. The series of ε_t is the white noise with unit variance, and $v_t = \sum_{s=1}^{t} \varepsilon_s$. We further write $T_1 = [T\tau_1]$ and $T_2 = [T\tau_2]$, where $1 \geq \tau_2 > \tau_1 \geq 0$. Then, for any τ_1 and τ_2, as $T \to \infty$,

$$\mathrm{diag}[T^{-1/2}I, T^{-3/2}I] \sum_{T_1}^{T_2} [h_t', g_t']'[h_t', g_t'] \,\mathrm{diag}[T^{-1/2}I, T^{-3/2}I] \\ \to \int_{\tau 1}^{\tau 2} [h(\tau)', g(\tau)']'[h(\tau)', g(\tau)']d\tau, \tag{5.4}$$

$$\mathrm{diag}[T^{-1/2}I, T^{-3/2}I] \sum_{T_1}^{T_2} [h_t', g_t']'[\varepsilon_t, v_t] \,\mathrm{diag}[1, T^{-1}] \\ \xrightarrow{w} \int_{\tau 1}^{\tau 2} [h(\tau)', g(\tau)']'[dB(\tau), B(\tau)d\tau]. \tag{5.5}$$

Note that $g(\tau) = \int_0^\tau h(\bar{\tau})d\bar{\tau}$. For instance, the continuous time representation of $\boldsymbol{du}(b)$ in (2.4) is 0 for $\tau \leq b$ and 1 for $\tau > b$. That of $\boldsymbol{dt}(b_j)$ in (2.13) is 0 for $\tau \leq b_j$ and $\tau - b_j$ for $\tau > b_j$. Let $m(\tau) = [g(\tau)', B(\tau)']'$, which is $(p+1) \times 1$, and

$$\tilde{m}(\tau) = m(\tau) - \int_0^1 m(\tau)h(\tau)'d\tau(\int_0^1 h(\tau)h(\tau)'d\tau)^{-1}h(\tau). \tag{5.6}$$

Tabulate the distribution of

$$(p+1)^{-1}\int_0^1 dB(\tau)\tilde{m}(\tau)'(\int_0^1 \tilde{m}(\tau)\tilde{m}(\tau)'d\tau)^{-1}\int_0^1 \tilde{m}(\tau)dB(\tau). \tag{5.7}$$

The upper α point in the distribution of (5.7) is adopted as the critical value of $UURT$.

Suppose that x in (5.3) is generated by

$$x = SH\mu + v, \tag{5.8}$$

$$\Delta x = H\mu + \Delta v, \tag{5.9}$$

where μ is a nonstochastic vector, and Δv is the data vector of the series of Δv_t that is a stationary $AR(k)$ (with zero mean). Then it is known that $UURT$ is distributed asymptotically as (5.7) indicates. As for the case where the series of Δv_t is a stationary ARMA satisfying Assumption 5.1, Said and Dickey (1984) and Ng and Perron (1995) show that if k in (5.3) goes to ∞ but $T^{-1/3}k$ goes to 0 as $T \to \infty$, (5.7) is still the limit distribution of $UURT$. On the other hand, suppose that the x in (5.3) is generated by

$$x = H\mu_0 + SH\mu_1 + u, \tag{5.10}$$

where μ_0 and μ_1 are nonstochastic, and the series of u_t is a stationary $AR(k+1)$ (with zero mean). Then it is known that $UURT$ diverges to ∞ as $T \to \infty$.

Henceforth we shall assume

Assumption 5.2 *ι is a column of H.*

We impose this assumption partly because it is most likely that ι is so chosen in empirical work, and partly because whether the data, X, is demeaned or not is made irrelevant by Assumption 5.2. This fairly obvious assertion can be derived from only the construction of the statistic, $UURT$, and does not depend on the DGPs of x in (5.3), even though our proof of the assertion will appear within the proof of Proposition 5.1 in Appendix A. As for (5.7), since an element of the vector function, h, is now the constant, 1, demeaning operations are embodied in (5.6).

The DGP of principal components given in the previous chapter differ from either (5.8) or (5.10). We shall investigate how the above test works on the principal components.

5.2 Group ⊥: The Case Where $B_\perp \eta_{\perp,i}$ is not a Cointegration Vector

Consider the principal component given in (4.3) and (4.4). Since $B_\perp \eta_{\perp,i}$ is not a cointegration vector, $X_S B_\perp \eta_{\perp,i}$ in (4.3) and $\Delta X_S B_\perp \eta_{\perp,i}$ in (4.4) correspond, respectively, to v in (5.8) and to Δv in (5.9). Although (4.3) has $SHQ\delta_{1i}$ and (4.4) has ζ_i, we can show that the above unit root test is applicable.

Proposition 5.1 *If x in* (5.3) *is generated by* (4.3) *and* (4.4) *with Assumptions 2.2 and 5.2, and if $\Delta X_S B_\perp \eta_{\perp,i}$ is a stationary AR(k) (with zero mean), the limit distribution of $UURT$ is given by the distribution of* (5.7).

Remark 5.1. The result of Said and Dickey (1984) and Ng and Perron (1995) is applicable. $\Delta X_S B_\perp \eta_{\perp,i}$ may be a stationary ARMA that satisfies Assumption 5.1.

It is easy to show that $SHQ\delta_{1i}$ is irrelevant. But the effect of ζ_i in (4.5) requires careful investigation. The quadratic form in the numerator of (5.3) must be $O_p(1)$ (weakly converging to (5.7) apart from multiplication by a constant) *even though it is not divided by T.* ζ_i introduces additional terms in the quadratic form. Appendix A shows proof of Proposition 5.1, indicating that the effect of ζ_i asymptotically vanishes by virtue of Definition 2.2(iv) in the context of Assumption 2.2.

5.3 Group ⊥: The Case Where $B_\perp \eta_{\perp,i}$ is a Cointegration Vector

Consider the principal component in (4.6) and (4.7). Here $X_S B_\perp \eta_{\perp,i}$ is stationary. Let us begin with the standard time series model, (5.10). To the best of our knowledge the literature has not been explicit about the divergence of $UURT$ in the case where u in (5.10) is a general stationary process, not necessarily $AR(k+1)$. Our investigation has disclosed that the divergence is related to the Martingale covariance to be given below. Suppose that the series of u_t is generated by a stationary, linear, indeterministic (in the Wold's sense [(8)]) process with zero mean. Given a positive integer, k, construct

$$\Delta\tilde{u}_t = \Delta u_t - \mathrm{E}(\Delta u_t \mid \Delta u_{t-1}, \ldots, \Delta u_{t-k}), \tag{5.11}$$

and

$$\tilde{u}_{t-1} = u_{t-1} - \mathrm{E}(u_{t-1} \mid \Delta u_{t-1}, \ldots, \Delta u_{t-k}). \tag{5.12}$$

Both $\Delta\tilde{u}_t \equiv 0$ and $\tilde{u}_{t-1} \equiv 0$ are excluded by the assumption made about u_t.

$$\mathrm{cov}(\Delta\tilde{u}_t, \tilde{u}_{t-1}) \tag{5.13}$$

will be called the Martingale covariance for the given k.

Lemma 5.1 *Suppose that x in* (5.3) *is generated by* (5.10) *with a stationary, linear, indeterministic u. Then UURT with lag order, k, diverges to ∞ if and only if the Martingale covariance on u for the k is not zero.*

Let us turn to the principal component, (4.6) and (4.7). Comparison between (4.6) and (5.10) shows that $SHQ\delta_{1i} + X_S B_\perp \delta_{2i}$ is in (4.6) but not in (5.10). Since $X_S B_\perp$ may be I(1) (but δ_{2i} is $O_p(T^{-1/2})$), its presence in (4.6) leads to asymptotic analyses that are substantially different from (5.10). Nevertheless we can show the following.

Lemma 5.2 *Suppose (a) that Assumptions 2.2 and 5.2 hold, (b) that x in* (5.3) *is generated by* (4.6) *and* (4.7), *and (c) that $X_S B_\perp \eta_{\perp,i}$ is stationary, linear, and indeterministic with zero mean. Then UURT with lag order, k, diverges to ∞ if and only if the Martingale covariance on $X_S B_\perp \eta_{\perp,i}$ for the k is not zero.*

In Section 5.8, the non-zero Martingale covariance will be transformed into an expression easier to interpret. If the series of u_t is a stationery $AR(k_*)$ and $k_* \leq k + 1$, the Martingale covariance for k is not zero. If the series of u_t is a stationary, indeterministic process, the Martingale covariance is not zero for sufficiently large k. Under Assumption 5.1, $X_S B_\perp \eta_{\perp,i}$ is an indeterministic process, which leads to the following result.

Proposition 5.2 *If x in* (5.3) *is generated by* (4.6) *and* (4.7) *with Assumptions 2.2, 3.1, 5.1, and 5.2, and if a sufficiently large k is chosen, then UURT diverges to ∞ as $T \to \infty$ at the speed of T.*

5.4 Group 2: The Case Where $r_2 = 1$, and Group 1

In the case of $r_2 = 1$ Group 2 has only one principal component, and the univariate unit root test, (5.3), is applied to the principal component.

Proposition 5.3 *Suppose that $r_2 = 1$. If x in* (5.3) *is given by* (4.8) *and* (4.9) *with Assumptions 2.2 and 5.2, and if $\Delta X_S B_2$ is $AR(k)$ with zero mean, then the limit distribution of UURT is given by the distribution of* (5.7).

An important point is that $\eta_{2,i}$ is a nonstochastic scalar constant, unity. The case where $r_2 \geq 2$ will be explained in Section 5.6.

In applying the unit root test to principal components of Group 1 we shall treat each component individually even when $r_1 \geq 2$. For the case where $r_1 = 1$ it is easy to show

Proposition 5.4 *Suppose that $r_1 = 1$ and that Assumptions 2.2, 5.1, and 5.2 hold. If x in* (5.3) *is given by* (4.10) *and* (4.11)*, then $UURT$ with a sufficiently large k diverges to ∞ at the speed of T.*

As for the case where $r_1 \geq 2$, even though $u \equiv X_S B_1 \eta_{1,i}$ with stochastic $\eta_{1,i}$ is not a standard time series, the analyses can proceed in the same way as in the proof of Lemma 5.2.

Proposition 5.5 *Suppose that $r_1 \geq 2$ and that Assumptions 2.2, 3.1, 5.1 and 5.2 hold. If x in* (5.3) *is generated by* (4.10) *and* (4.11)*, then $UURT$ for any k a.s. diverges to ∞ as $T \to \infty$ at the speed of T.*

5.5 Multivariate Unit Root Test

A multivariate extension of (5.3) and (5.7) appears in Inoue (1999) and Johansen et al. (2000). Let x_t' be a d-variate time series. The d-dimensional unit root test statistic with lag order, k, is constructed on the series of x_t as follows. Let, for $i = 0, \ldots, k$,

$$\Delta X_{-i} = [\Delta x_{k-i+2}, \ldots, \Delta x_{T-i}]', \quad (T-k-1) \times d,$$

$$X_{-1} = [x_{k+1}, \ldots, x_{T-1}]', \quad (T-k-1) \times d,$$

$$Z = [H, \Delta X_{-1}, \ldots, \Delta X_{-k}], \quad (T-k-1) \times (p + (kd)), \tag{5.14}$$

and we write $\Delta X = \Delta X_0$. Calculate

$$MURT \equiv (T-k-1) S_{00}^{-1/2} S_{01} S_{11}^{-1} S_{10} S_{00}^{-1/2\prime}, \tag{5.15}$$

where

$$S_{00} = (T-k-1)^{-1} \Delta X'(I - P(Z)) \Delta X, \tag{5.16}$$

$$S_{01} = (T-k-1)^{-1} \Delta X'(I - P(Z))[SH, X_{-1}], \tag{5.17}$$

and

$$S_{11} = (T-k-1)^{-1} [SH, X_{-1}]'(I - P(Z))[SH, X_{-1}]. \tag{5.18}$$

The test statistic is either the maximum eigenvalue or the trace of $MURT$. These statistics are invariant through any choice of non-unique $S_{00}^{-1/2}$ in (5.15) in so far as

$$S_{00}^{-1/2} S_{00} S_{00}^{-1/2\prime} = I.$$

This is because all eigenvalues of $S_{00}^{-1/2} S_{01} S_{11}^{-1} S_{10} (S_{00}^{-1/2})'$ are the roots of $\det[S_{01} S_{11}^{-1} S_{10} - \lambda S_{00}] = 0$. $MURT$ is the abbreviation of multivariate unit root test.

Regarding the limit distribution, let $B(\tau)$ be the d-dimensional standard Brownian motion, and construct

$$M(\tau) = [g(\tau)', B(\tau)']', \quad (p + r_2) \times 1,$$

and

$$\tilde{M}(\tau) = M(\tau) - \int_0^1 M(\tau) h(\tau)' d\tau (\int_0^1 h(\tau) h(\tau)' d\tau)^{-1} h(\tau).$$

What are fitted to the maximum eigenvalue and trace of $MURT$ are the distributions of the maximum eigenvalue and trace of

$$\int_0^1 dB(\tau) \tilde{M}(\tau)' (\int_0^1 \tilde{M}(\tau) \tilde{M}(\tau)' d\tau)^{-1} \int_0^1 \tilde{M}(\tau) dB(\tau)', \tag{5.19}$$

respectively. This is a test of zero cointegration rank in Johansen et al. (2000).

Let us consider a linear transformation of x_t' into $\tilde{x}_t'$.

Lemma 5.3 *Let* $\tilde{x}_t' = x_t' G^{-1}$, *where G may be stochastic so far as it is a.s. nonsingular. Let* $\tilde{S}_{00}$, $\tilde{S}_{01}$, *and* $\tilde{S}_{11}$ *be* (5.16), (5.17), *and* (5.18) *with* $\tilde{X}$ *substituted for X and* $\tilde{Z} = [H, \Delta\tilde{X}_{-1}, \ldots, \Delta\tilde{X}_{-k}]$ *for Z. Then*

$$S_{00}^{-1/2} S_{01} S_{11}^{-1} S_{10} S_{00}^{-1/2\prime} \text{ and } \tilde{S}_{00}^{-1/2} \tilde{S}_{01} \tilde{S}_{11}^{-1} \tilde{S}_{10} \tilde{S}_{00}^{-1/2\prime}$$

share the same eigenvalues.

Since our test statistics are constructed by the eigenvalues of

$$S_{00}^{-1/2} S_{01} S_{11}^{-1} S_{10} S_{00}^{-1/2\prime},$$

we can conclude that the data may be linearly transformed without affecting the multivariate unit root test.

Regarding the relation between $MURT$ and $UURT$ suppose that $(I - \boldsymbol{P}(Z))$ in the denominator of $UURT$ is replaced by $(I - \boldsymbol{P}(Z_0))$, where Z_0 and Z are given in (5.1) and (5.2). Then $UURT$ would be a special case of $MURT$ such that $d = 1$ (apart from $(p+1)^{-1}$ and the degree of freedom of $\Delta x'(I - \boldsymbol{P}(Z_0))\Delta x$).[(9)]

In Johansen et al. (2000) the DGP of the series of x_t in (5.15) is the cointegrated VAR model involving linear deterministic trends subjected to structural changes. (5.15) is the statistic to test for the zero cointegration rank on the likelihood based inference method. We are applying the statistic, (5.15), to a DGP different from theirs.

5.6 Group 2: The Case Where $r_2 \geq 2$

The multivariate unit root test is applied to the entire set of principal components of Group 2 when $r_2 \geq 2$. $S_{00}^{-1/2}$ may be obtained by the Cholesky decomposition of S_{00}. We introduce

Assumption 5.3 *(i) The DGP of $X_S B_2$ is such that*

$$\Delta B_2' s_t = \Gamma_1 \Delta B_2' s_{t-1} + \cdots + \Gamma_k \Delta B_2' s_{t-k} + \varepsilon_t,$$

where the sequence of ε_t is a r_2-dimensional white noise with mean zero and a positive definite covariance matrix, Λ. (ii) $I - \Gamma_1 L - \cdots - \Gamma_k L^k$ is stable.

Assumption 5.3(ii) above is required because $X_S B_2$ should not be cointegrated.

Proposition 5.6 *Suppose that $r_2 \geq 2$ and that Assumptions 2.2, 5.3, and 5.2 hold with a given k. If MURT with the lag order, k, is calculated on the set of r_2 principal components,* (4.8) *and* (4.9), *the limit distributions of the maximum eigenvalue and trace of MURT are the distributions of the maximum eigenvalue and trace, respectively, of* (5.19).

One may wonder how the univariate unit root test statistic would behave if it *were* applied to an individual component series of (4.8) and (4.9) when $r_2 \geq 2$. The analysis is possible in the special case where $\Delta X_S B_2$ is a vector white noise and (5.3) is calculated with $k = 0$. We do not obtain the limit distribution, (5.7). The analysis seems difficult in the general case.

5.7 Mistaken Constituents of Groups

5.7.1 Mistaken Constituents of Groups 2 and 1

In the DGP Group 2 consists of $i = n - r + 1, \ldots, n - r + r_2 (= n - r_1)$, and Group 1 of $i = n - r_1 + 1, \ldots, n$.

(i) A type of mistaken constituents is $i = n-r+1, \ldots, n-r_1, n-r_1+1, \ldots, n-r_1+h$ for Group 2, and $i = n-r_1+h+1, \ldots, n$ for Group 1, where $h > 0$. Some components that in fact belong to Group 1 is allocated to Group 2 (Group 2 in the DGP may be null, i.e., r_2 may be zero). If the mistaken Group 2 consists of a single principal component, we would be interested in the univariate unit root test applied to it. If the mistaken Group 2 contains more than one principal component, we would be interested in the multivariate unit root test applied to the set of these components. We would also be interested in the univariate unit root test applied to each individual principal component in the mistaken Group 1, but its result is obvious because the component belongs to the Group 1 in the DGP as well. Therefore, we shall consider below the mistaken Group 2 only. When $r_2 + h > 1$ the mistaken Group 2 contains more than one principal component. The multivariate unit root test is applied to the principal components, $(I - \boldsymbol{P}(\iota))X[\hat{\xi}_{n-r+1}, \dots, \hat{\xi}_{n-r_1}, \hat{\xi}_{n-r_1+1}, \dots, \hat{\xi}_{n-r_1+h}]$. The first r_2 columns are in Group 2 in the DGP, while the last h columns are in Group 1 in the DGP. S_{00} is $(r_2 + h) \times (r_2 + h)$, and S_{11} is $(p + r_2 + h) \times (p + r_2 + h)$.

Proposition 5.7 *Suppose that Assumptions 2.2, 5.1, 5.3, and 5.2 hold, and that X in $MURT$ has r_2+h columns, of which the first r_2 columns are given by* (4.8) *and* (4.9), *and the last h columns by* (4.10) *and* (4.11). *Then the first,..., the h-th eigenvalues (in descending order) of $MURT$ diverge to ∞ as $T \to \infty$ at the speed of T.*

The unit root hypothesis, i.e., zero cointegration rank, is rejected in regard to the mistaken Group 2 in probability 1 if T is sufficiently large. When $r_2 = 0$ and $h = 1$ so that the mistaken Group 2 has only one component that belongs to Group 1 of the DGP, the univariate unit root test statistic diverges because of Propositions 5.4 and 5.5. Comparing the above results with Proposition 5.6, we see the unit root test is useful to discern the mistaken constituents of Groups 2 and 1 from the correct constituents in the present case.

(ii) Another type of mistaken constituents is $i = n-r+1, \dots, n-r_1-h$ for Group 2, and $i = n-r_1-h+1, \dots, n$ for Group 1. $h > 0$, and $r_2-h \geq 1$. Some components that in fact belong to Group 2 are allocated to Group 1. We are interested in the univariate unit root test applied to each individual principal component of the mistaken Group 1. Unfortunately, we are unable to determine the distribution of $UURT$ applied to the component, $(I - \boldsymbol{P}(\iota))X\hat{\xi}_{n-r_1-h+i}$, $i = 1, \dots, h$, in Group 2. We are also interested in either the univariate or the multivariate unit root test applied to the mistaken Group 2. Again we do not know the distributions of the test statistic applied to a subset of principal components of Group 2 in the DGP. We cannot discern the mistaken constituents from the correct constituents in the present case.

5.7.2 Mistaken Constituents of Group $\perp$ and Group 2

In the DGP the Groups $\perp$ and 2 are, respectively, $i = 1, \ldots, n-r$ and $i = n-r+1, \ldots, n-r+r_2$.

(i) A type of mistaken constituents is to include in Group 2 some principal components that belong to Group $\perp$ of the DGP. The Groups $\perp$ and 2 of the mistaken constituents are, respectively, $i = 1, \ldots, n-r-h$, and $i = n-r-h+1, \ldots, n-r, \ldots, n-r+r_2$. $h > 0$. We are interested in the univariate or multivariate unit root test applied to the mistaken Group 2, and also the univariate unit root test applied to each individual principal component in the mistaken Group $\perp$. Since the mistaken Group $\perp$ is a subset of Group $\perp$ in the DGP, Sections 5.2 and 5.3 are applicable to individual principal components of the mistaken Group $\perp$. Therefore, we shall consider the mistaken Group 2 only. When $r_2 + h > 1$ so that the mistaken Group 2 has more than one principal component, the result of the multivariate unit root test applied to them depends on whether at least one of $B_\perp \eta_{\perp,n-r-h+1}, \ldots, B_\perp \eta_{\perp,n-r}$, or none of them, is in the cointegration space.

Proposition 5.8 *Suppose that X in $MURT$ is such that the columns other than the first h are* (4.8) *and* (4.9). *If all of the first h columns are* (4.3) *and* (4.4), *$MURT$ is asymptotically distributed as* (5.19). *If at least one of the first h columns are* (4.6) *and* (4.7), *$MURT$ diverges.*

When the mistaken Group 2 has only one component, which is in Group $\perp$ in the DGP, Proposition 5.2 is applicable. The unit root tests are useful to discern the present mistaken constituents from the correct one, when and only when $B_\perp \eta_{\perp,i}$ is a cointegration vector for one of those i's which are in Group $\perp$ but erroneously allocated to Group 2.

(ii) Another type of mistaken constituents is to include in Group $\perp$ some components that belong to Group 2 in the DGP so that $i = 1, \ldots, n-r, n-r+1, \ldots, n-r+h$ for Group $\perp$, and $i = n-r+h+1, \ldots, n-r_1$ for Group 2. We are interested in the unit root test applied to the mistaken Group 2, but we are unable to determine the limit distribution of the test statistic on a subset of the principal components of Group 2 in the DGP. We cannot discern the mistaken constituents from the correct ones by the unit root tests.

5.8 Supplement on the Martingale Covariance

Consider a stationary, indeterministic process, u_t, with zero mean. Let $\gamma_j = \mathrm{E}(u_t u_{t-j})$ and construct

$$\Gamma_{(k+1)} = \begin{bmatrix} \gamma_0 & \gamma_1 & \cdots & \gamma_k \\ \gamma_1 & \gamma_0 & \cdots & \gamma_{k-1} \\ \vdots & \vdots & \ddots & \vdots \\ \gamma_k & \gamma_{k-1} & \cdots & \gamma_0 \end{bmatrix},$$

$$\gamma_{(k+1)} = [\gamma_1, \gamma_2, \ldots, \gamma_{k+1}]', \text{ and } \tau_{k+1} = \iota_{k+1}' \Gamma_{(k+1)}^{-1} \gamma_{(k+1)}, \tag{5.20}$$

where ι_{k+1} is a $(k+1) \times 1$ vector of one. τ_{k+1} is the sum of the coefficients in the projection of u_t upon $[u_{t-1}, \ldots, u_{t-k-1}]$.

Lemma 5.4 *In the stationary, linear, indeterministic process with zero mean the Martingale covariance,* (5.13), *is zero if and only if* $\tau_{k+1} = 1$.

The reality of $\tau_{k+1} = 1$ will be considered. (i) If the series of u_t is $AR(k+1)$ so that

$$u_t = a_1 u_{t-1} + \cdots + a_{k+1} u_{t-k-1} + \varepsilon_t,$$

then $\Gamma_{(k+1)}^{-1} \gamma_{(k+1)} = [a_1, \ldots, a_{k+1}]'$. Since $1 > a_1 + \cdots + a_{k+1}$, we have $\tau_{k+1} < 1$. (ii) The same result follows when u is $AR(k_*)$ and $k_* < k+1$. (iii) If $k_* > k+1 \geq 3$, we cannot exclude the possibility that $\tau_{k+1} = 1$. However, we think it is a very exceptional case in terms of reality. (iv) If the series of u_t is $AR(\infty)$ after inverting its MA part so that

$$u_t = a_1 u_{t-1} + a_2 u_{t-2} + \cdots + \varepsilon_t$$

with the sequence of $|\, a_j \,|$ bounded by a decaying exponential,

$$1 > \sum_{j=1}^{\infty} a_j = \tau_\infty.$$

When k is sufficiently large, the contribution of $[u_{t-k-2}, u_{t-k-3}, \ldots]$ to the projection of u_t on $[u_{t-1}, u_{t-2}, \ldots]$ is sufficiently small, i.e., $|\, \tau_k - \tau_\infty \,|$ is sufficiently small. Thus $\tau_k < 1$ if k is sufficiently large.

6 Trend Tests

The following two major points, (a) and (b), have emerged in the previous chapter.

(a) The principal components such that the unit root test statistic, $UURT$, diverges are either in Group 1, or in Group $\perp$ where $B_\perp \eta_{\perp,i}$ is a cointegration vector. Although the statistic in both groups diverges, principal components in Group 1 do not have a deterministic trend and those in Group $\perp$ have a deterministic trend of order $O(T^{3/2})$.

(b) The principal components such that either $UURT$ or $MURT$ has the limit distribution are either in Group 2, or in Group $\perp$ where $B_\perp \eta_{\perp,i}$ is not a cointegration vector. Although the statistics in both groups have the limit distributions, principal components in Group 2 do not have a deterministic trend and those in Group $\perp$ have a deterministic trend of order $O(T^{3/2})$.

In this chapter, we consider procedures to determine whether or not principal components have deterministic trends of order $O(T^{3/2})$ for each case (a) and (b).

The plan of this chapter is as follows. Section 6.1 will present our trend test in cases where the unit root test statistic diverges. The procedure exploits differences of order among the principal components. They are of order $O(T^{3/2})$ when a deterministic trend exists, while they are of order $O(T^{1/2})$ when a deterministic trend does not exist. In cases where the unit root tests have the limit distribution, to determine whether or not principal components have deterministic trends requires a great deal of effort. Section 6.2 will show that the conventional F test does not work on our principal components because they contain some minor, nonstandard terms. In Section 6.3 an ad hoc method is adopted, and its limiting distribution is derived in absence of deterministic trends. Because the limit distribution involves a unknown matrix parameter, csp(Q), the reduced rank regression of X on SH is calculated with a number of alternatively chosen ranks in order to derive "estimates" of the parameter. This regression method is described in Section 6.4, and its properties are analysed in Sections 6.5 and 6.6. Substitution of an "estimate" of csp(Q) into the limiting distribution makes the critical value data-dependent, and this will be analysed in Section 6.7. In Section 6.8, we shall analyse the effects on trend tests which incorrect divisions among Group $\perp$, Group 2, and Group 1 would bring about.

6.1 Discrimination Between Group 1 and Group $\perp$ with $B_{\perp}\eta_{\perp,i}$ as a Cointegration Vector

Although the dominating term of the principal components expressed in (4.6) is one of the demeaned common deterministic trends of order $O(T^{3/2})$, they also include minor but complicated terms. The two major terms of order $O_p(T^{1/2})$ in the principal components expressed in (4.10) also have complicated structures. $\eta_{1,i}$ in (4.10) is stochastic and, in addition, the projection of X_{D*} onto $X_S B_2$ requires special attention.(10) Because both principal components in (4.6) and (4.10) have complicated structures, we try to discriminate them with the use of a large discrepancy in their orders. Because principal components in (4.10) lack not only the common trends of order $O(T^{3/2})$ but also any terms of order $O_p(T)$, they are at most of order $O_p(T^{1/2})$. On the other hand, principal components in (4.6) are of order $O(T^{3/2})$. Let x_T be a principal component either in (4.6) or (4.10), a be a real number such that $3 > a > 1$, T_0 be a given positive integer, and x_{T0} be the vector that consists of the initial T_0 elements of x_T. If x_T is (4.6), $T^{-a}x_T'x_T$ diverges to infinity as $T \to \infty$. The probability that

$$T^{-a}x_T'x_T - T_0^{-a}x_{T0}'x_{T0} \tag{6.1}$$

is positive can be made as close to 1 as we wish by taking T sufficiently large. If x_T is (4.10), $T^{-a}x_T'x_T$ converges to zero as $T \to \infty$. The probability that (6.1) is negative can be made as close to 1 as we wish by taking T sufficiently large.

Proposition 6.1 *The sign of* (6.1) *discriminates (a) the principal component in Group* $\perp$ *such that* $B_{\perp}\eta_{\perp,i}$ *is a cointegration vector and (b) the principal component in Group 1 correctly with probability 1 if* T *is sufficiently large.*

The choice of a and T_0 will be considered in simulation studies in Chapter 8. Let us move on to the next discrimination.

6.2 Failure of the Standard Trend Tests in Discriminating Groups $\perp$ and 2

The principal components in Group 2 are $O_p(T)$, while the principal components in Group $\perp$ are $O_p(T^{3/2})$. Because the discrepancy in orders is small between the two groups, we cannot expect that the discrimination strategy above would work in the length of time series data that are used in macroeconomic studies. One might turn to the differenced series of principal components, i.e., the expressions, (4.4) and (4.9). Since (4.4) does, and (4.9) does not contain H, we might try to test the significance of the coefficient vector of H. $\Delta X_S B_\perp \eta_{\perp,i}$ in (4.4) and $\Delta X_S B_2 \eta_{2,i}$ in (4.9) are both differenced series of I(1) variables. Consider the simple case, $r_2 = 1$, so that $\eta_{2,i}$ is the scalar, 1. Let us consider a regression equation in which the dependent variable is the differenced principal component to be denoted by Δz, and the independent variables are $[H, \Delta z_{-1}, \ldots, \Delta z_{-k}]$. One can construct the F statistic to test for significance of the coefficient vector of H. Unfortunately, this attempt does not succeed. ζ_i in (4.4), in particular, $HQ\delta_5$ in (4.5), complicates the null distribution of the F statistic. (The statistic is asymptotically a quadratic form of $T^{-1/2}H'\varepsilon + T^{-1/2}H'HQ\delta_5$. Both terms are $O_p(1)$. The first term is standard, contributing to the χ^2 distribution, but the second term is not standard.) A kind of F statistic with z as the dependent variable and $[SH, z_{-1}, \ldots, z_{-k}]$ as the independent variable is even worse. It diverges on the principal components of Group 2 by virtue of the terms included in $O_p(T^{1/2})$ on the RHS of (4.8).

6.3 Test Statistic and Limit Distribution for the Discrimination Between Group 2 and Group $\perp$ with $B_\perp \eta_{\perp,i}$ not in the Cointegrating Space

For the data matrix of a d-dimensional vector time series, Z, $T \times d$, we shall use

$$TRT \equiv (Z'(I - \boldsymbol{P}([H, SH]))Z)^{-1/2} Z'\boldsymbol{P}([H, SH])Z(Z'(I - \boldsymbol{P}([H, SH]))Z)'^{-1/2}, \quad (6.2)$$

where for convenience we let

$$Z'(I - \boldsymbol{P}([H, SH]))Z = (Z'(I - \boldsymbol{P}([H, SH]))Z)^{1/2}(Z'(I - \boldsymbol{P}([H, SH]))Z)'^{1/2}$$

be the Cholesky decomposition. H and SH are, respectively, the demeaned H and SH. TRT has been motivated as follows. If Z contains $[H, SH]$, the middle term of (6.2),

$$Z'\boldsymbol{P}([H, SH])Z$$

and hence (6.2) itself diverge, while if Z does not contain $[H, SH]$, (6.2) remains bounded. The test statistic is either the maximum eigenvalue or the trace of TRT. TRT is the abbreviation of trend test. The invariance of eigenvalues through the linear transformation of data, such as Lemma 5.3, also holds on TRT.

Let us consider the case where Z is the r_2 vectors of principal components in Group 2.

Proposition 6.2 *Suppose in* (6.2) *that* $d = r_2$ *and* Z *is* (4.8) *over* $i = 1, \ldots, r_2$. *Then the maximum eigenvalue and trace of* TRT *weakly converge to the maximum eigenvalue and trace, respectively, of*

$$(V_0 - V_1)^{-1/2}(V_1 - V_2)(V_0 - V_1)'^{-1/2} \tag{6.3}$$

where

$$V_0 = \int_0^1 \tilde{B}(\tau)\tilde{B}(\tau)'d\tau, \tag{6.4}$$

$$V_1 = \int_0^1 \tilde{B}(\tau)[\tilde{h}(\tau)', \tilde{g}(\tau)']d\tau(\int_0^1 [\tilde{h}(\tau)', \tilde{g}(\tau)']'[\tilde{h}(\tau)', \tilde{g}(\tau)']d\tau)^{-1} \times \int_0^1 [\tilde{h}(\tau)', \tilde{g}(\tau)']'\tilde{B}(\tau)'d\tau, \tag{6.5}$$

$$V_2 = \int_0^1 \tilde{B}(\tau)\tilde{g}(\tau)'Qd\tau(\int_0^1 Q'\tilde{g}(\tau)\tilde{g}(\tau)'Qd\tau)^{-1} \int_0^1 Q'\tilde{g}(\tau)\tilde{B}(\tau)'d\tau. \tag{6.6}$$

Q *has been defined in* (4.1). $\tilde{B}(\tau)$ *is the* r_2*-dimensional demeaned standard Brownian motion process, and* $\tilde{h}(\tau)$ *and* $\tilde{g}(\tau)$ *are the continuous time representations of the demeaned* H *and demeaned* SH*, respectively.*

The reason why Q is involved in the distribution is that the principal components in Group 2, (4.8), contain $(I - \boldsymbol{P}(SHQ))X_S B_2$. The numerator of (6.2) converges to $V_1 - V_2$ with Q in V_2 because of the following identity

Lemma 6.1

$$(I - \boldsymbol{P}(SHQ))\boldsymbol{P}([H, SH])(I - \boldsymbol{P}(SHQ)) = \boldsymbol{P}([H, SH]) - \boldsymbol{P}(SHQ).$$

Q in (6.6) poses the major problem to be resolved in the rest of the present chapter. It is important to note here that (6.6) depends not on Q itself but on csp(Q). If H were not included in the set on which the projection is made in (6.2), $\tilde{h}'$ would not be in V_1. Without $\tilde{h}'$ (6.3) would be zero in the case where $p = n - r$, because Q is then square and nonsingular, making $V_1 = V_2$. This would complicate our test of significance of trend.

Let us turn to the case where TRT is calculated on the individual principal components in Group $\perp$. Here we need not distinguish $B_\perp \eta_{\perp,i}$ being and not being a cointegration vector.

Proposition 6.3 *Suppose in* (6.2) *that* $d = 1$ *and* Z *is one of the individual principal components in Group* $\perp$, (4.3) *or* (4.6). *Then* TRT *diverges to* ∞ *as* $T \to \infty$. *The speed of divergence is* T *in* (4.3) *and* T^2 *in* (4.6).

6.4 Reduced Rank Regression of X on SH

The sections through Section 6.6 will present analyses of the reduced rank regression of X on SH to estimate csp(Q) in (6.6). The regression method is described in the present Section 6.4, and the properties of the estimate will be analysed in the subsequent Sections 6.5 and 6.6. It is important to emphasise here that what should be estimated is not Q itself but csp(Q).

Using the notations in (2.2), (2.8), (4.1), and (4.2), we have

$$X = X_{D\perp} + X_{D*} + X_S = SHQB'_{\perp} + HK + X_S + O(1).$$

SHQ is $O(T^{3/2})$ while the remainder is $O_p(T)$. This leads us to a reduced rank regression of X on SH because $\text{rank}(QB'_{\perp}) = \text{rank}(Q) = n - r \leq p$ (see Definition 2.2(ii)), while $QB'_{\perp}$ is $p \times n$. Since $n - r$ is a unknown parameter, we shall try a number of ranks, q, in the reduced rank regression, i.e., q is an integer variable such that $1 \leq q \leq \min(p, n) \equiv q_{max}$. In the context of the reduced rank regression $B'_{\perp}$ will be replaced by a more natural notation, R'. Let $\tilde{Q}$ and $\tilde{R}'$ be, respectively, $p \times q$ and $q \times n$ matrix variables, and consider for a given q the minimisation of

$$\det[(X - SH\tilde{Q}\tilde{R}')'(I - \boldsymbol{P}(\iota))(X - SH\tilde{Q}\tilde{R}')]$$

subject to the condition that $\text{rank}(\tilde{Q}) = \text{rank}(\tilde{R}') = q$. When the minimum is attained at $\tilde{Q} = \hat{Q}$ and $\tilde{R}' = \hat{R}'$, $\hat{Q}\hat{R}'$ is called the reduced rank regression coefficient, with rank, q, in the regression of X on SH. Given q, one cannot uniquely determine $\hat{Q}$ and $\hat{R}'$ separately, but the determination of $\hat{Q}\hat{R}'$ is unique. When $q = q_{max}$, the reduced rank regression is identical to the OLS, no matter whether $p > n$ or $p \leq n$. When the rank, q, should be made explicit, we shall write $\hat{Q}_{(q)}\hat{R}'_{(q)}$.

Hereafter, X and SH will denote the demeaned X and SH. A standard method to calculate $\hat{Q}\hat{R}'$ is as follows (see, for example, Johansen (1988)). Cholesky decompose $H'S'SH$ as

$$H'S'SH = (H'S'SH)^{1/2}(H'S'SH)'^{1/2}.$$

Denote the inverse of $(H'S'SH)^{1/2}$ and $(H'S'SH)'^{1/2}$ respectively by $(H'S'SH)^{-1/2}$ and $(H'S'SH)'^{-1/2}$. Construct

$$RRR = (H'S'SH)^{-1/2}H'S'X(X'X)^{-1}X'SH(H'S'SH)'^{-1/2}. \tag{6.7}$$

$\text{rank}(X) = n$, and $\text{rank}(SH) = p$. The rank of RRR is $\min(p, n)$, and the eigenvalues are $\tilde{\lambda}_1 > \cdots > \tilde{\lambda}_{q_{max}} > 0$. It can be shown that $1 \geq \tilde{\lambda}_1$. Let $\tilde{\xi}_1, \ldots, \tilde{\xi}_{q_{max}}$ be the orthonormalised eigenvectors that correspond to $\tilde{\lambda}_1, \ldots, \tilde{\lambda}_{q_{max}}$. Given q, the result of the reduced rank regression is

$$\hat{Q}_{(q)}\hat{R}'_{(q)} = (H'S'SH)'^{-1/2}[\tilde{\xi}_1,\ldots,\tilde{\xi}_q][\tilde{\xi}_1,\ldots,\tilde{\xi}_q]'(H'S'SH)^{-1/2}H'S'X.$$

Even though $\hat{Q}_{(q)}$ and $\hat{R}'_{(q)}$ are not unique, it will be found convenient to set

$$\hat{Q}_{(q)} = (T^{-3}H'S'SH)'^{-1/2}[\tilde{\xi}_1,\ldots,\tilde{\xi}_q], \tag{6.8}$$

$$\hat{R}'_{(q)} = [\tilde{\xi}_1,\ldots,\tilde{\xi}_q]'(T^{-3}H'S'SH)^{-1/2}T^{-3}H'S'X. \tag{6.9}$$

We shall focus on (6.8), while keeping in mind that our concern is with csp($\hat{Q}_{(q)}$). When q is chosen equal to $n - r$, csp($\hat{Q}_{(n-r)}$) may be regarded as an estimate of csp(Q) in the DGP of X. But $n - r$ is unknown, and the situations $q > n - r$, $q = r$, and $q < n - r$ all have to be investigated in our analyses of $\hat{Q}_{(q)}$. Notice that X enters into (6.7) only through $\boldsymbol{P}(X)$. Our analyses will proceed in two steps. In the first step to be given in Section 6.5, RRR is modified by replacing $\boldsymbol{P}(X)$ in it by an expression approximately equal to the RHS of (3.15). This will enable us to perform an exact, finite sample analysis of the eigenvectors of the modified RRR. In the second step to be given in Section 6.6, $\boldsymbol{P}(X)$ is recovered, and Proposition 3.4 is used to turn the results in the first step into the asymptotic results on the eigenvectors of the original RRR. This completes our analysis of $\hat{Q}$ because it does not depend on X directly (as $\hat{R}'$ does).

6.5 A Finite Sample Analysis of the Reduced Rank Regression

Define $Y_\perp$, Y_2, and Y_1 by

$$Y_\perp \equiv SHQ, \tag{6.10}$$

$$Y_2 \equiv (I - \boldsymbol{P}(SHQ))X_S B_2, \tag{6.11}$$

$$Y_1 \equiv (I - \boldsymbol{P}(SHQ) - \boldsymbol{P}((I - \boldsymbol{P}(SHQ))X_S B_2))(X_{D*} + X_S)B_1, \tag{6.12}$$

where Q, $p \times (n - r)$, is that of the DGP of X. Noting that $Y_\perp \perp Y_2 \perp Y_1$, write $Y = [Y_\perp, Y_2, Y_1]$. Since what matters hereafter is not Q itself but csp(Q), we shall assume without losing generality that $Q'Q = I_{n-r}$. Using (4.1) and (4.2), it is seen that the three terms on the RHS of (3.15) are related to $Y_\perp$, Y_2, and Y_1, respectively, as follows.

$$\boldsymbol{P}(X_D B_\perp) \approx \boldsymbol{P}(Y_\perp), \tag{6.13}$$

$$\boldsymbol{P}((I - \boldsymbol{P}(X_D B_\perp))X_S B_2) \approx \boldsymbol{P}(Y_2), \tag{6.14}$$

$$\boldsymbol{P}((I - \boldsymbol{P}(X_D B_\perp) - \boldsymbol{P}((I - \boldsymbol{P}(X_D B_\perp))X_S B_2)XB_1) \approx \boldsymbol{P}(Y_1), \tag{6.15}$$

where the meaning of $\approx$ has been given in Section 3.5. Then it follows from Proposition 3.4 that $\boldsymbol{P}(X) \approx \boldsymbol{P}(Y)$. Noting that $\boldsymbol{P}(X)$ is involved in the middle part of the RHS of (6.7), let us replace it by $\boldsymbol{P}(Y)$. It leads to

$$(H'S'SH)^{-1/2}H'S'\boldsymbol{P}(Y)SH(H'S'SH)'^{-1/2}. \tag{6.16}$$

Just as the eigenvectors of (6.7) are involved in the expression for $\hat{Q}_{(q)}$, (6.8), the eigenvectors of (6.16) will be substituted in (6.8).

T is fixed in the rest of the present section. Either $p > n - r$ or $p = n - r$. (See Definition 2.2(ii) and the remark at the end of Section 2.2.) If $p = n - r$, $Q = I$, and $\text{csp}(SH) = \text{csp}(SHQ)$. For the case where $p > n - r$ we wish to construct the orthogonal complement of $\text{csp}(SHQ)$ within $\text{csp}(SH)$. Let $Q_\perp$ be $p \times (p - n + r)$ with rank, $p - n + r$, such that $Q'_\perp Q = 0$ and $Q'_\perp Q_\perp = I_{p-n+r}$, so that $[Q, Q_\perp]$ is an orthogonal matrix. Construct

$$Q_* = Q_\perp - Q(Q'H'S'SHQ)^{-1}Q'H'S'SHQ_\perp, \tag{6.17}$$

which is $p \times (p - n + r)$. Then $SHQ_* = (I - \boldsymbol{P}(SHQ))SHQ_\perp$ has full column rank, and

$$SHQ \perp SHQ_*, \quad \boldsymbol{P}(SH) = \boldsymbol{P}(SHQ) + \boldsymbol{P}(SHQ_*). \tag{6.18}$$

Let $U_2 = Y_2(Y_2'Y_2)^{-1/2}$, $U_1 = Y_1(Y_1'Y_1)^{-1/2}$, and $U = [U_2, U_1]$. Then $U'U \equiv I_r$. Our analyses of (6.16) will need the eigenvalues and eigenvectors of $U'\boldsymbol{P}(SHQ_*)U$. From (6.10), (6.11), and (6.12) it follows that

$$U'SHQ = 0. \tag{6.19}$$

SHQ_* and U each have their full column ranks. Because of (6.19) the random space, $\text{csp}(U)$, lies within $\text{csp}(I - \boldsymbol{P}(SHQ))$. So does $\text{csp}(SHQ_*)$. However, it is not possible to choose a nonstochastic γ so that $Q_*'H'S'U\gamma = 0$ a.s. From these points it can be derived that the rank of $U'\boldsymbol{P}(SHQ_*)U$ is $\min(\text{rank}(SHQ_*), \text{rank}(U))$, where $\text{rank}(SHQ_*) = p - n + r$, and $\text{rank}(U) = r$. We have an identity that $\min(p - n + r, r) = q_{max} - n + r$, where $q_{max} = \min(p, n)$. Therefore, the rank of $U'\boldsymbol{P}(SHQ_*)U$ is $q_{max} - n + r$ ($q_{max} - n + r \geq 0$ in general). We emphasise that $U'\boldsymbol{P}(SHQ_*)U$ exists only if $q_{max} > n - r$. Let Λ_* be the diagonal matrix of the $q_{max} - n + r$ positive eigenvalues of $U'\boldsymbol{P}(SHQ_*)U$ in the descending order, and Ω_*, $r \times (q_{max} - n + r)$, be the matrix of eigenvectors that correspond to these eigenvalues. $\Omega_*'\Omega_* = I_{q_{max}-n+r}$. Then $U'\boldsymbol{P}(SHQ_*)U = \Omega_*\Lambda_*\Omega_*'$.

Lemma 6.2

(i) *The positive eigenvalues of* (6.16) *consist of (a)* 1 *with* $n-r$ *multiplicity and (b) if* $q_{max} > n-r$*, the positive eigenvalues of* $U'\mathbf{P}(SHQ_*)U$. *Those in (b) are a.s. less than* 1.

(ii) *The ortho-normalised eigenvectors of* (6.16) *that correspond to the eigenvalue, 1, are*

$$\xi_{\perp} = (H'S'SH)'^{1/2}Q(Q'H'S'SHQ)'^{-1/2}\Omega_{\perp}, \tag{6.20}$$

where $(Q'H'S'SHQ)'^{-1/2}$ *is defined through the Cholesky decomposition, and* $\Omega_{\perp}$ *is an arbitrary* $(n-r)\times(n-r)$ *nonstochastic orthogonal matrix.*

(iii) *The ortho-normalised eigenvectors that correspond to the eigenvalues less than* 1 *and arranged in the descending order are*

$$\xi_* = (H'S'SH)^{-1/2}Q_{\perp}Q_*'H'S'U\Omega_*\Lambda_*^{-1/2}. \tag{6.21}$$

$\Omega_{\perp}$ in (6.20) originates in the multiplicity of the eigenvalue, 1.

The expression, (6.8), involves the eigenvectors of (6.7), $\xi_1,\ldots,\xi_q$, but the expression may be calculated with the eigenvectors of (6.16) that have been obtained in Lemma 6.2. The result should be denoted by a symbol different from $\hat{Q}_{(q)}$, but we shall use the same symbol.

Lemma 6.3 *Concerning* $\hat{Q}_{(q)}$, $q = 1,\ldots,q_{max}$, *in* (6.8) *calculated from the eigenvectors of* (6.16) *rather than* (6.7), *we would have the following result.*

(i) *When* $q = n-r$,

$$\hat{Q}_{(n-r)} = Q(T^{-3}Q'H'S'SHQ)'^{-1/2}\Omega_{\perp}. \tag{6.22}$$

(ii) *When* $q < n-r$,

$$\hat{Q}_{(q)} = Q(T^{-3}Q'H'S'SHQ)'^{-1/2}C_{\perp}, \tag{6.23}$$

where $C_{\perp}$ *is a* $(n-r)\times q$ *nonstochastic matrix that is arbitrary except for* $C_{\perp}'C_{\perp} = I_q$.

(iii) *When* $q > n-r$,

$$\hat{Q}_{(q)} = [\hat{Q}_{(n-r)}, \Gamma[I_{q-n+r}, 0']'], \tag{6.24}$$

where

$$\Gamma = Q_*(T^{-3}Q_*'H'S'SHQ_*)^{-1}T^{-3/2}Q_*'H'S'U\Omega_*\Lambda_*^{-1/2}$$

and 0 *is* $(q_{max}-q)\times(q-n+r)$.

In (6.22) $\hat{Q}_{(n-r)}$ is not uniquely determined because of indeterminate $\Omega_\perp$ in (6.20), but csp($\hat{Q}_{(n-r)}$) is uniquely determined because two different $\Omega_\perp$ are related through a post-multiplication by a $(n-r)\times(n-r)$ nonsingular matrix. In (6.23) even csp($\hat{Q}_{(q)}$) is not uniquely determined because two different $C_\perp$ are not related through a post-multiplication by a $q \times q$ nonsingular matrix. In (6.24) Γ is stochastic, but $\Gamma[I_{q-n+r}, 0']'$ is free from the kind of indeterminateness that $\hat{Q}_{(n-r)}$ has. csp($\hat{Q}_{(q)}$) in (6.24) is a uniquely determined random space.

6.6 Asymptotic Analyses of the Reduced Rank Regression

We now return to RRR in (6.7), and $P(Y)$ is reverted back to $P(X)$. $\hat{Q}_{(q)}$ in (6.8) is constructed by the eigenvector of RRR. Asymptotic properties of csp($\hat{Q}_{(q)}$), $q = 1, \ldots, q_{max}$, will be investigated in relation to csp(Q). While Q and $Q_\perp$ are parameters given in the DGP of X, Q_* in (6.17) varies as T does. The asymptotic version of (6.17) is needed to transform the above finite sample analysis to the asymptotic. When $p > n - r$, define

$$\begin{bmatrix} N_{11} & N_{12} \\ N_{12}' & N_{22} \end{bmatrix} = \lim_{T\to\infty} T^{-3}[Q, Q_\perp]'H'S'SH[Q, Q_\perp]$$

and construct $Q_* = Q_\perp - QN_{11}^{-1}N_{12}$, which does not depend on T. Then

$$\lim_{T\to\infty} T^{-3}(SHQ_*)'SHQ = 0,$$

which is the asymptotic version of (6.18), and

$$N_{**} \equiv N_{22} - N_{12}'N_{11}^{-1}N_{12} = \lim_{T\to\infty} T^{-3}Q_*'H'S'SHQ_*$$

is positive definite if $p > n - r$. Transfer the notations, U_{22}, U_{11}, $G_{\perp\perp}$, $W_{2\perp}$, W_{12} and $G_{1\perp}$ from Chapter 3. See (3.5), (3.10), and (3.11). Define W_{*2} and G_{*1} by

$$T^{-5/2}Q_*'H'S'X_SB_2 \xrightarrow{w} W_{*2} \text{ and } T^{-2}Q_*'H'S'X_{D*}B_1 \to G_{*1}.$$

Then

$$\begin{aligned} T^{-3/2}Q_*'H'S'U &= [T^{-5/2}Q_*'H'S'Y_2(T^{-2}Y_2'Y_2)^{-1/2}, T^{-2}Q_*'H'S'Y_1(T^{-1}Y_1'Y_1)^{-1/2}] \\ &\xrightarrow{w} [W_{*2}U_{22}^{-1/2}, W_{*1}U_{11}^{-1/2}] \equiv V_*, \end{aligned}$$

where $W_{*1} = G_{*1} - W_{*2}[U_{22}^{-1}, -U_{22}^{-1}W_{2\perp}G_{\perp\perp}^{-1}][W_{12}, W_{1\perp}]'$. $U'P(SHQ_*)U$ weakly converges to a random matrix, $V_*'N_{**}^{-1}V_*$. What Ω_* and Λ_* converge to will also be written Ω_* and Λ_*.

Because of Proposition 3.4 and (6.13) through (6.15), the difference between (6.7) and (6.16) is $O_p(T^{-1/2})$. Notations for the eigenvalues and eigenvector of (6.7) were given below (6.7). From Lemma 6.2(i) it follows that $\tilde{\lambda}_1, \ldots, \tilde{\lambda}_{n-r}$ converge jointly to 1, and also that $\tilde{\lambda}_{n-r+1}, \ldots, \tilde{\lambda}_{q_{max}}$ converge to the eigenvalues of $V_*' N_{**}^{-1} V_*$, which are a.s. less than 1.[11] As for the eigenvectors, they lacked a unique representation in the finite sample analysis of (6.16), because $\Omega_\perp$ in (6.22) is an arbitrary orthogonal matrix. Even though the eigenvectors of (6.7) do not have this indeterminateness for a finite T, the difference between the eigenvectors of (6.7) and (6.16) converges to zero as $T \rightarrow \infty$. We should recall that what should be estimated is csp(Q) rather than Q. The uniqueness of csp($\hat{Q}_{(q)}$) was not prevented by the indeterminateness of eigenvectors of (6.16) in the cases where $q = n - r$ and where $q > n - r$.

As we seldom deal with a limiting procedure in the sequence of vector spaces indexed by T, let us begin with some general considerations. Let X_T, $T = 1, 2, \ldots$, be a sequence of stochastic matrices, each $m \times n$, that is $O_p(1)$. $X_T \gamma$ is not $o_p(1)$ for any γ ($\neq 0$), but the sequence of X_T may not converge in any sense. (i) Suppose for a $m \times n$ nonstochastic matrix, A, with rank(A) = n, that $(I - \boldsymbol{P}(A))X_T$ converges in probability to zero. Then we say that csp(X_T) is asymptotically contained in csp(A). Suppose that the following condition holds in addition to (i) above, namely (ii) for an arbitrary $m \times \tilde{n}$ nonstochastic matrix $\tilde{A}$ (csp($\tilde{A}$) $\neq$ csp(A)) with rank($\tilde{A}$) = $\tilde{n} \leq n$, $(I - \boldsymbol{P}(\tilde{A}))X_T$ does not converge to zero in probability. Then we say that the sequence of random spaces, csp(X_T), converges in probability to csp(A).

Q, $p \times (n - r)$, is a parameter in the DGP, and csp(Q) is unique though Q is not. $\hat{Q}_{(q)}$, $q = 1, \ldots, q_{max}$, are the Q in the reduced rank regressions of X on SH. (6.8) has been chosen as $\hat{Q}_{(q)}$, which are now calculated from RRR in (6.7) rather than (6.16).

Proposition 6.4

(i) *When* $q = n - r$, $\hat{Q}_{(n-r)} = Q N_{11}'^{-1/2} \Omega_\perp + O_p(T^{-1/2})$, *and the sequence of* csp($\hat{Q}_{(n-r)}$) *converges in probability to* csp(Q).

(ii) *When* $q < n - r$, csp($\hat{Q}_{(q)}$), *having q dimensions, is asymptotically contained in* csp(Q), *but we cannot say that the sequence of* csp($\hat{Q}_{(q)}$) *converges.*

(iii) *When* $q > n - r$, *the sequence of* csp($\hat{Q}_{(q)}$) *converges to*

$$\text{csp}(Q) + \text{csp}(Q_\perp N_{**}^{-1} V_* \Omega_* \Lambda_*^{-1/2} [I_{q-n+r}, 0']').$$

Concerning (i), $\text{plim}_{T\to\infty}(I - \boldsymbol{P}(Q))\hat{Q}_{(n-r)} = 0$ for any $\Omega_\perp$, while for any $p \times \tilde{n}$ nonstochastic $\tilde{Q}$ (csp(Q) $\neq$ csp($\tilde{Q}$)) with rank($\tilde{Q}$) = $\tilde{n} \leq n - r$, $\text{plim}_{T\to\infty}(I - \boldsymbol{P}(\tilde{Q}))\hat{Q}_{(n-r)}$

is not zero for any $\Omega_\perp$. As for (ii), when $q < n - r$, $\hat{Q}_{(q)} = QN_{11}'^{-1/2}C_\perp + O_p(T^{-1/2})$ so that $\text{plim}_{T\to\infty}(I - P(Q))\hat{Q}_{(q)} = 0$. In (iii) the two column spaces are mutually orthogonal, and + means formation of the algebraic union of vector spaces. (iii) will be proved in Appendix A.[12]

6.7 Data-Dependent Critical Value

In the rest of the present chapter we shall investigate the performance of the trend test implemented by $\hat{Q}_{(q)}$, $q = 1, \ldots, q_{max}$, substituted into Q in (6.6). Fix Q in (6.6) at the value of one of $\hat{Q}_{(q)}$ obtained from the given data, X, and consider the upper α point in the distribution of (6.3). We shall attempt to use this point as though it were the critical value in the trend test with TRT in (6.2). If q is chosen equal to $n-r$, our test is asymptotically equivalent to the test that we would do if csp(Q) were known. This will be shown in the present section. The cases where q is chosen otherwise will be investigated in Section 6.8.

Let us examine what is involved in (6.3). $[\tilde{h}', \tilde{g}']$ are fixed through our consideration, and will not be shown explicitly in the following notations. The dimension of $\tilde{B}$ will be denoted by $d(\tilde{B})$. csp(Q) and $d(\tilde{B})$ are two important factors that determine the distribution of (6.3). We may proceed with either the maximum eigenvalue or the trace of (6.3), but the maximum eigenvalue will be adopted below. The expression (6.3) is denoted by $M(Q, d(\tilde{B}))$ and its maximum eigenvalue by $\lambda_1(M(Q, d(\tilde{B})))$. The upper α point in the distribution of $\lambda_1(M(Q, d(\tilde{B})))$ will be denoted by $C_Q(\alpha, d(\tilde{B}))$. When $\hat{Q}_{(q)}$ is substituted for Q in (6.6), (6.3) is $M(\hat{Q}_{(q)}, d(\tilde{B}))$, and its maximum eigenvalue is $\lambda_1(M(\hat{Q}_{(q)}, d(\tilde{B})))$. The distribution of $\lambda_1(M(\hat{Q}_{(q)}, d(\tilde{B})))$ can be tabulated while fixing $\hat{Q}_{(q)}$ at the value calculated from the data. What generates this distribution is the probability measure of $\tilde{B}$, the demeaned Brownian motion. The upper α point in this distribution will be denoted by $\hat{C}_{(q)}(\alpha, d(\tilde{B}))$. It is a random variable in terms of the probability measure of X_S, from which $\hat{Q}_{(q)}$ has been calculated. With a given q our trend test is implemented, using $\hat{C}_{(q)}(\alpha, d(\tilde{B}))$ as though it were the critical value for the significance level, α. The trend is judged absent if the maximum eigenvalue of TRT in (6.2) with $d = d(\tilde{B})$ does not exceed $\hat{C}_{(q)}(\alpha, d(\tilde{B}))$, and judged present otherwise. $\hat{C}_{(q)}(\alpha, d(\tilde{B}))$ will be called the data-dependent critical value.

Lemma 6.4 *Let q_1 and q_2 be positive integers such that $q_1 < q_2$. Suppose that $\hat{Q}_{(q_1)}$ and $\hat{Q}_{(q_2)}$ are obtained from the same data, X. Then*

$$\hat{C}_{(q_1)}(\alpha, d(\tilde{B})) > \hat{C}_{(q_2)}(\alpha, d(\tilde{B})).$$

The same $(\alpha, d(\tilde{B}))$ is used on both sides in the equation above, but $d(\tilde{B})$ may be arbitrary. This result holds true in probability 1 in the probability measure of X_S.

We shall consider the role of q within the framework of hypothesis-testing to see if constituents of three Groups, $\perp$, 2, and 1 are consistent with the data. This testing is our ultimate goal as announced in Section 3.6. A hypothetical assignment of constituents of the three groups will be called the hypothesised grouping. Two kinds of tests, (a) and (b), will be performed with TRT in (6.2). (a) Principal component(s) in Group 2 in the hypothesised grouping is (are) substituted for Z in (6.2). The data-dependent critical value is derived with $\hat{Q}_{(q)}$ where q is the number of constituents in Group $\perp$ in the hypothesised grouping. The reason why this number is chosen for q is that it is $n-r$ if the hypothesised grouping is identical to the grouping in the DGP. The dimension of $\tilde{B}$ is equal to the number of principal components in Group 2. (b) Consider the principal components in Group $\perp$ on which unit roots have been found. They are substituted in (6.2) individually. The data-dependent critical value is the same as above, i.e., q is the number of constituents in Group $\perp$ in the hypothesised grouping. The dimension of $\tilde{B}$ is 1.

We shall investigate the performance of the above tests, (a) and (b), in various relations between the hypothesised grouping and the grouping in the DGP. The case where the two groupings are identical means in effect that the true grouping is known, and it will be examined below within the present section. The case where the two groupings differ will be investigated in the next Section, 6.8.

Suppose that the true grouping is known so that Group $\perp$ consists of $i = 1, \ldots, n-r$, and Group 2 of $i = n-r+1, \ldots, n-r+r_2$. Initially we consider applying the trend test, (6.2), to the principal components in Group 2 so that $d = r_2$. Since $n-r$ is assumed known, we would implement the reduced rank regression of X on SH with $q = n-r$. Therefore suppose that Q in (6.6) is replaced by $\hat{Q}_{(n-r)}$. The trend test at the significance level, α, is made with $\hat{C}_{(n-r)}(\alpha, r_2)$. Earlier in Proposition 6.2 the unknown Q was used in (6.6) as though it were known. In comparison we have the following result.

Proposition 6.5 *Suppose that $n-r$ is known but* csp(Q) *is not.*

(i) $\hat{C}_{(n-r)}(\alpha, r_2) - C_Q(\alpha, r_2)$ *is* $O_p(T^{-1/2})$.

(ii) The maximum eigenvalue of TRT, (6.2), *on the $n-r+1$-th,...,$n-r+r_2$-th principal components exceeds $\hat{C}_{(n-r)}(\alpha, r_2)$ in the probability that is asymptotically equal to α as $T \to \infty$.*

The trend would not be found in the principal components of Group 2 in the probability that is asymptotically equal to $1 - \alpha$.

Secondly we consider applying the trend test to an individual principal component in Group $\perp$ such that $B_{\perp}\eta_{\perp,i}$ is not a cointegration vector. Here $d = 1$, and the maximum eigenvalue of (6.2) is (6.2) itself. Again $\hat{Q}_{(n-r)}$ is substituted in Q in (6.6), but, since $d = 1$, the critical value is $\hat{C}_{(n-r)}(\alpha, 1)$. The trend test compares (6.2) with $\hat{C}_{(n-r)}(\alpha, 1)$.

Proposition 6.6 *Suppose that* $n - r$ *is known but* $\text{csp}(Q)$ *is not.*

(i) $\hat{C}_{(n-r)}(\alpha, 1) - C_Q(\alpha, 1)$ *is* $O_p(T^{-1/2})$.

(ii) TRT, *(6.2), diverges, and hence exceeds* $\hat{C}_{(n-r)}(\alpha, 1)$ *in probability 1 as* $T \to \infty$ *when applied to an individual principal component of Group* $\perp$ *such that* $B_{\perp}\eta_{\perp,i}$ *is not a cointegration vector.*

The trend would be found.

6.8 Mistaken Constituents of the Groups ⊥ and 2

We shall consider the case where the hypothesised grouping differs from the grouping in the DGP, i.e., the hypothesised grouping is mistaken.

6.8.1 Constituents of Group ⊥ Mistaken for Group 2

The constituents of the groups in the DGP are the same as before, but suppose that one has mistaken Group $\perp$ as $i = 1, \ldots, n - r - h$, where $h > 0$, and Group 2 as $i = n - r - h + 1, \ldots, n - r - h + r_a$, where $r_a \geq 0$. If $-h + r_a \leq 0$, the mistaken Group 2 consists entirely of the principal components in Group $\perp$ of the DGP. If $r_2 \geq -h + r_a > 0$, the mistaken Group 2 consists of h components of Group $\perp$ and some components of Group 2 of the DGP. If $-h + r_a > r_2$, the mistaken Group 2 contains, in addition, some principal components of Group 1 of the DGP.

(i) Initially we consider applying the trend test to the mistaken constituents of Group 2. Z in (6.2) consists of the $(n - r - h + 1)$-th,..., $(n - r - h + r_a)$-th principal components so that $d = r_a$. When one erroneously assumes Group $\perp$ as $i = 1, \ldots, n - r - h$, the reduced rank regression of X on SH would be run with $q = n - r - h$. One would replace Q in (6.6) by $\hat{Q}_{(n-r-h)}$. Therefore the data-dependent critical value would be $\hat{C}_{(n-r-h)}(\alpha, r_a)$. The trend test compares the maximum eigenvalue of TRT, (6.2), with $\hat{C}_{(n-r-h)}(\alpha, r_a)$.

Proposition 6.7 *Suppose that* $n - r$ *is mistaken for* $n - r - h$. *(*$h > 0$*)*

(i) $\hat{C}_{(n-r-h)}(\alpha, r_a)$ *is bounded.*

(ii) *The maximum eigenvalue of* TRT, (6.2), *on the* $(n-r-h+1)$*-th,...,*$(n-r-h+r_a)$*-th principal components diverges as* $T \to \infty$.

The trend would be found in the mistaken constituents of Group 2. Comparing Proposition 6.5 and Proposition 6.7 we can discern the mistaken constituents of Groups $\perp$ and 2 in the present case from the correct constituents in the DGP.

(ii) Let us consider the case where the trend test is applied to an individual principal component of mistaken Group $\perp$. Z in (6.2) is one of the first,..., $(n-r-h)$-th principal components. Since Group $\perp$ is erroneously assumed as $i = 1, \ldots, n-r-h$, $\hat{Q}_{(n-r-h)}$ is substituted in Q in (6.6) to derive the data-dependent critical value. The test compares TRT with $\hat{C}_{(n-r-h)}(\alpha, 1)$. By virtue of Proposition 6.3 TRT diverges, while $\hat{C}_{(n-r-h)}(\alpha, 1)$ is bounded. Then the trend would be found.

6.8.2 Constituents of Group 2 Mistaken for Group $\perp$

The constituents of groups in the DGP are the same as before, but suppose that one has mistaken Group $\perp$ as $i = 1, \ldots, n-r, n-r+1$, and Group 2 as $i = n-r+2, \ldots, n-r+r_2$. We shall consider this restricted setting of mistaken constituents because no definitive result has been obtained as will be shown below.

(i) Assuming that $r_2 \geq 2$, let us consider applying the trend test to the mistaken Group 2, setting Z in (6.2) as the $(n-r+2)$-th,...,$(n-r+r_2)$-th principal components so that $d = r_2 - 1$. Since the mistaken Group $\perp$ is $i = 1, \ldots, n-r, n-r+1$, $\hat{Q}_{(n-r+1)}$ is substituted in (6.6) to obtain the data-dependent critical value. The test compares the maximum eigenvalue of TRT in (6.2) with $\hat{C}_{(n-r+1)}(\alpha, r_2 - 1)$. The question is whether $\hat{C}_{(n-r+1)}(\alpha, r_2 - 1)$ is larger or smaller than the true α point in the distribution of the maximum eigenvalue of TRT. The $(n-r+2)$-th,..., $(n-r+r_2)$-th principal components are

$$Z = (I - P([\iota, SHQ]))X[\hat{\xi}_{n-r+2}, \ldots, \hat{\xi}_{n-r+r_2}],$$

deleting $\hat{\xi}_{n-r+1}$. Let $[\hat{\eta}_{2,1}, \hat{\eta}_{2,2}, \ldots, \hat{\eta}_{2,r_2}]$ be the orthonormalised eigenvectors (listed in the order that corresponds to the descending order of eigenvalues) of

$$T^{-2}B_2'\tilde{X}_S'(I - P(\tilde{X}_D B_\perp))\tilde{X}_S B_2,$$

where $\tilde{X}_D$ and $\tilde{X}_S$ are demeaned X_D and X_S. ($\hat{\eta}_{2,i}$ weakly converges to $\eta_{2,i}$.) Define $\hat{\eta}_2 \equiv [\hat{\eta}_{2,2}, \ldots, \hat{\eta}_{2,r_2}]$ deleting $\hat{\eta}_{2,1}$. Then it can be shown by Lemma 6.1 that (a) the largest eigenvalue of (6.2) with the above Z and (b) the largest root of λ in

$$\det[\tilde{\eta}_2' B_2' \tilde{X}_S'(P([H, SH]) - P(SHQ))\tilde{X}_S' B_2 \tilde{\eta}_2 \\ - \lambda \tilde{\eta}_2' B_2' \tilde{X}_S (I - P([H, SH]))\tilde{X}_S B_2 \tilde{\eta}_2] = 0. \quad (6.25)$$

are asymptotically identical. Q in (6.25) is that in the DGP. $\tilde{X}_S B_2 \tilde{\eta}_2$ cannot be represented by a standard time series model, and the asymptotic distribution of the largest root of (6.25) is hard to derive in general. What *may* be close to (6.25) is

$$\det[(V_1 - V_2) - \lambda(V_0 - V_1)] = 0, \quad (6.26)$$

where V_0, V_1, and V_2 are constructed as in (6.4), (6.5), and (6.6) with $d(\tilde{B}) = r_2 - 1$ and the Q in the DGP substituted in (6.6). In comparing (6.25) and (6.26) notice that with any $(r_2 - 1) \times (r_2 - 1)$ positive definite matrix, Γ, the LHS of (6.26) can be premultiplied by $\det[\Gamma^{1/2}]$ and postmultipled by $\det[\Gamma'^{1/2}]$ without affecting the roots of λ. The roots of (6.26) are equivalent to the eigenvalues of (6.3). Therefore, the previously defined $C_Q(\alpha, r_2 - 1)$ is the upper α point in the distribution of the largest root of (6.26). By virtue of Proposition 6.4(iii), $M(Q, r_2 - 1) - M(\hat{Q}_{(n-r+1)}, r_2 - 1)$ is asymptotically positive semidefinite, and $\lambda_1(M(Q, r_2 - 1)) \geq \lambda_1(M(\hat{Q}_{(n-r+1)}, r_2 - 1))$ in probability 1. Therefore,

$$C_Q(\alpha, r_2 - 1) \geq \hat{C}_{(n-r+1)}(\alpha, r_2 - 1). \quad (6.27)$$

Noting that the RHS is the critical value used in the present test, (6.27) leads to a *conjecture* that we may reject an absence of trend in a probability larger than α.

(ii) Another trend test that may be conducted in the present mistaken constituents of Group $\perp$ and Group 2 is TRT on one of the mistaken Group $\perp$, the $(n - r + 1)$-th principal component, so that $d = 1$. This statistic is compared with $\hat{C}_{(n-r+1)}(\alpha, 1)$. The analysis of the statistic must distinguish the case where $r_2 = 1$ and the case where $r_2 > 1$ in the DGP. In the case where $r_2 = 1$ the $(n - r + 1)$-th principal component is the sole component of Group 2 in the DGP. It is approximately

$$(I - P([\iota, SHQ]))X_S B_2,$$

where B_2 is $n \times 1$ nonstochastic. Proposition 6.2 is applicable. The limit distribution of TRT is (6.3) with $d(\tilde{B}) = 1$ and Q in the DGP. Its α point is $C_Q(\alpha, 1)$. As shown in Proposition 6.5(i) $\hat{C}_{(n-r)}(\alpha, 1)$ converges to $C_Q(\alpha, 1)$, but as shown in Lemma 6.4 $\hat{C}_{(n-r+1)}(\alpha, 1)$ is smaller than $\hat{C}_{(n-r)}(\alpha, 1)$. The probability that TRT exceeds $\hat{C}_{(n-r+1)}(\alpha, 1)$ is larger than α. When $r_2 > 1$ the $(n - r + 1)$-th principal component is approximately

$$(I - P([\iota, SHQ]))X_S B_2 \eta_{2,1}$$

where $\eta_{2,1}$ is $n \times 1$ stochastic. The limiting distribution of TRT with this Z is not known. The conclusion is that the mistaken constituents of Group $\perp$ and Group 2 in the present case cannot be discerned from the correct constituents in the DGP.

7 Sequential Decision Rule

We are now ready to consider how to determine $n - r$, r_2, and r_1. In Chapter 3 $i = 1, \ldots, n$ is the running index to denote the *descending* order of eigenvalues of the data covariance matrix. i is also associated with the principal component that corresponds to the i-th eigenvalue. Given $n - r$, r_2, and r_1, the principal components with $i = 1, \ldots, n - r$, with $i = n - r + 1, \ldots, n - r + r_2 \equiv n - r_1$, and with $i = n - r_1 + 1, \ldots, n$ each reveal asymptotically distinctive features. Thus $i = 1, \ldots, n$ has been divided in three groups, Group $\perp$ that consists of $i = 1, \ldots, n - r$, Group 2 that consists of $i = n - r + 1, \ldots, n - r + r_2 \equiv n - r_1$, and Group 1 that consists of $i = n - r_1 + 1, \ldots, n$.

7.1 Grouping Method

By the grouping method we shall mean the drawing of borders between Group $\perp$ and Group 2, and between Group 2 and Group 1. Determination of $n - r$, r_2, and r_1 is equivalent to selection of a particular grouping method from the list of all possible ones. A grouping method will be denoted, for example, as Group $\perp$= [1], Group 2 = [2, 3], and Group 1 = "null". The integer within [$\cdot$] indicates the i used above, i.e., the ordering indices of principal components. In the above example, $n = 3$ so that 3 principal components are allocated among 3 Groups. The Group $\perp$ contains the first principal component only as indicated by [1]. Group 2 consists of the second and the third principal components as indicated by [2, 3]. Group 1 has none.

In considering all possible grouping methods we must delete from the list those which are not consistent with the results of analyses in Chapters 2 and 3. Table 7.1 gives three examples of grouping methods that are not consistent. (a) is not acceptable because the Arabic number in [$\cdot$] for Group 2 should be smaller than that for Group 1. The eigenvalues that reveal the property of Group 2 exceed in size, and hence precede in the order the eigenvalues that reveal the property of Group 1. When $n = 3$ and $p = 2$, (b) of Table 7.1 is unacceptable, because $n - r \leq p$

Table 7.1. Grouping methods inconsistent with the theory

(a)	Group ⊥ = [1]	Group 2 = [3]	Group 1 = [2]
(b)	Group ⊥ = [1,2,3]	Group 2 = "null"	Group 1 = "null"
(c)	Group ⊥ = "null"	[1,2,3] is allocated between Groups 2 and 1	

Table 7.2. Ordering of grouping methods $n = 3$, $p = 2$

Grouping method (1):	Group ⊥=[1]	Group 2=[2, 3]	Group 1="null"
Grouping method (2):	Group ⊥=[1]	Group 2=[2]	Group 1=[3]
Grouping method (3):	Group ⊥=[1]	Group 2="null"	Group 1=[2, 3]
Grouping method (4):	Group ⊥=[1, 2]	Group 2=[3]	Group 1="null"
Grouping method (5):	Group ⊥=[1, 2]	Group 2="null"	Group 1=[3]

Note: Group ⊥= [1, 2, 3] is inadmissible.

by Definition 2.2(ii), and $n - r$ is the number of principal components in Group ⊥, which cannot exceed $p = 2$. (c) of Table 7.1 is inadmissible because $n - r = 0$ is excluded by Assumption 2.1.

All of the grouping methods that are consistent with the results in Chapters 2 and 3 will be *ordered* by the following two principles, (i) and (ii). (i) The grouping method that contains a smaller number of principal components in Group ⊥ precedes the grouping method that contains a larger number of principal components in Group ⊥. (ii) Between those grouping methods that share the identical principal components in Group ⊥ the grouping method that contains a larger number of principal components in Group 2 precedes the grouping method that contains a smaller number of principal components in Group 2. For example, when $n = 3$ and $p = 2$, there exist five grouping methods that are consistent with the results in Chapters 2 and 3, and they are ordered as indicated in Table 7.2. The first three grouping methods have only one principal component in Group ⊥, while the last two grouping methods have two in Group ⊥. By the principle (i) introduced above, the first three precede the last two. The first three grouping methods share the same list of principal component, [1]. As specified by the principle (ii), the grouping method that has two components in Group 2 precedes the grouping method that has one in Group 2, which in turn precedes the grouping method that has none in Group 2. The last two grouping methods share the identical list of principal components, $[1, 2]$, in Group $\perp$. As specified by the principle (ii), the grouping method that has one component in Group 2 precedes the grouping method that has none in Group 2.

We shall use the running index, j, to denote the ordering of the grouping methods, placing it in $(\cdot)$. Thus, the second grouping method is denoted as (2). In general, the number of grouping methods that are consistent with the results of Chapters 2 and 3 is $jmax \equiv n + (n-1) + \cdots + (n-p+1)$. The first n grouping methods have $[1]$ in Group $\perp$. The next $n-1$ grouping methods have $[1, 2]$ in Group $\perp$. The last $n-p+1$ grouping method has $[1, \ldots, p]$.

7.2 Sequential Decision Rule

Out of the $jmax$ grouping methods, we wish to select one on the basis of available data. We adopt the following decision rule. First, test to see if the data of the principal components is consistent with what we should expect on the unit root and the trend tests if the grouping method (1) represents the grouping in the DGP. If it is consistent, accept the grouping method (1) and determine $n-r$, r_2, and r_1 accordingly. If it is not, test to see if (2) is consistent with what we should expect if (2) represents the grouping in the DGP. Continue this in the order of $(2), \ldots, (jmax)$ until we reach the grouping method that can be accepted. This will be called the *sequential decision rule.*

7.3 Tests of a Grouping Method

A given grouping method is tested as follows. The constituents of each of Groups $\perp$, 2, and 1, as specified by the given grouping method, are investigated to see if the results of unit root and trend tests are consistent with what we should expect if the constituents represent those of the DGP. If the results on any one of Groups $\perp$, 2, and 1 are not consistent, the given grouping method is rejected.

(1) In dealing with the principal components in Group $\perp$, the unit root test and the trend test are applied to individual series of principal components other than the first. (The tests are not applied to the first principal component because it always belongs to Group $\perp$. If Group $\perp = [1]$ the following explanation is irrelevant.) The unit root test uses the statistic, $UURT$ in (5.3). The trend test uses either TRT in (6.2) with $d = 1$ or (6.1), depending on the result of the unit root test. (6.2) with $d = 1$ is used when a unit root is found, while (6.1) is used when it is not. If a trend is not found in any one of the principal components in Group $\perp$, the grouping method

under investigation should be rejected. If a trend is found in all the principal components in Group $\perp$, the grouping method is accepted in so far as the constituents of Group $\perp$ are concerned.

(2) The procedures on the principal component(s) in Group 2 begin with the unit root test. If unit root(s) is (are) not found the grouping method under investigation should be rejected. On the other hand, if unit root(s) is (are) found there, we move to the trend test based on TRT in (6.2). If trend(s) is (are) found the grouping method under investigation must be rejected. If trend(s) is (are) not found the grouping method is accepted in so far as the constituents of Group 2 are concerned. Concrete procedures depend on whether Group 2 contains only one principal component or more than one principal component. When it contains only one, the unit root test uses $UURT$ in (5.3), and the trend test uses TRT in (6.2) with $d = 1$. If Group 2 contains more than one principal component, they should be treated jointly. The unit root test uses $MURT$ in (5.15), testing the hypothesis that the cointegration rank is zero, and the trend test uses TRT, (6.2).

(3) Investigation of principal components in Group 1 begins with the unit root test, applying $UURT$ in (5.3) to an individual principal component in Group 1. If a unit root is found in any one of the principal components, the grouping method under investigation must be rejected. If a unit root is not found we move on to the trend test, using (6.1). If a trend is found in any one of the principal components, the grouping method under investigation should be rejected. If a trend is not found, the grouping method is accepted in so far as the constituents of Group 1 are concerned.

Concerning the cases where the tests based on TRT in (6.2) are conducted, the distribution, (6.3), involves the unknown parameter, Q, in (6.6). The reduced rank regression of X on SH is run with that particular rank, q, which is consistent with the grouping method. For example, in the case where $n = 3$ and $p = 2$ as shown in Table 7.2, the number of common trends is 1 in the grouping methods (1) through (3), and q is set to 1. The number of common trends is 2 in the grouping methods (4) and (5), and q is 2. The estimate, $\hat{Q}_{(q)}$, in (6.8) with q so chosen is substituted for Q in (6.6).

If it were known that the grouping method, (j), represents the grouping in the DGP, the probability that this grouping method is accepted can be determined properly by controlling α used in each test. This holds even when $\hat{Q}_{(n-r)}$ with $n-r$ in (j) is substituted for Q as suggested above. The relevant earlier results are listed below.

- Unit root test in Group $\perp$: Proposition 5.1 for the case where $B_\perp \eta_{\perp,i}$ is not a cointegration vector, and Proposition 5.2 for the case where $B_\perp \eta_{\perp,i}$ is a cointegration vector;
- Trend test in Group $\perp$: Proposition 6.6(ii) for the case where $B_\perp \eta_{\perp,i}$ is not a cointegration vector, and Proposition 6.1 for the case where $B_\perp \eta_{\perp,i}$ is a cointegration vector;
- Unit root test in Group 2: Proposition 5.3 for the case where $r_2 = 1$, and Proposition 5.6 for the case where $r_2 \geq 2$;
- Trend test in Group 2: Proposition 6.5(ii);
- Unit root test in Group 1: Propositions 5.4 and 5.5;
- Trend test in Group 1: Proposition 6.1.

7.4 Justification of the Sequential Decision Rule

The sequential decision rule given above is justified by the following proposition.

Proposition 7.1 *Suppose that the grouping method, (j), represents the grouping in the DGP $(j = 1, \ldots, jmax)$. When $j \geq 2$, each of the grouping methods,* $(1), \ldots, (j-1)$ *is rejected in probability* 1 *if T is sufficiently large.*

Remark. When $j = 1$ so that (1) represents the grouping method in the DGP, (1) is accepted in a sufficiently high probability. It will be shown in Section 8.3.3 that we should accept $(jmax)$ if and only if all of $(1), (2), \ldots, (jmax - 1)$ are rejected.

Proof. Suppose that we test the grouping method, (j'), where $j' < j$.

(a) Initially we consider the case where (j) and (j') share the identical principal components in their Group $\perp$. The grouping method, (j), has $[1, \ldots, n-r]$, $[n-r+1, \ldots, n-r+r_2]$, and $[n-r_1+1, \ldots, h]$, respectively, as Group $\perp$, Group 2, and Group 1. On the other hand the grouping method, (j'), has $[1, \ldots, n-r]$, $[n-r+1, \ldots, n-r_1, n-r_1+1, \ldots, n-r_1+h]$, and $[n-r_1+h+1, \ldots, n]$, respectively, as Group $\perp$, Group 2, and Group 1. $h > 0$ because $j' < j$. The difference between (j) and (j') is seen only in regard to the border between Group 2 and Group 1. Group 2 of (j') is not null. When $r_2 = 0$ and $h = 1$, Group 2 of (j') contains only one principal component, which is in Group 1 in the DGP. The unit root test is based on $UURT$ in (5.3). As indicated in Proposition 5.4, the unit root is rejected in probability 1 for a sufficiently large T. When $r_2 + h \geq 2$, Group 2 of (j') contains more than one principal components, and the unit root test is based on $MURT$ in (5.15). But h principal components of Group 2 of (j') belong to Group 1 in the DGP. As indicated in (i) of Section 5.7.1, in particular, Proposition 5.7, the unit roots, i.e., zero cointegration rank, are rejected in probability 1 if T is sufficiently large. Rejection of unit roots in Group 2 of (j') necessarily leads to rejection of the grouping method, (j').

(b) Secondly we consider the case where the principal components in Group $\perp$ of (j') are a portion of those in Group $\perp$ of (j). Since $j' < j$ the set of principal components in Group $\perp$ of (j') cannot be larger than the set of principal components in Group $\perp$ of (j), and the case where the two sets are identical has been considered in (a) above. The constituents of (j) remain the same as above, but the constituents of (j') here are $[1, \ldots, n-r-h]$, $[n-r-h+1, \ldots, n-r-h+r_a]$, and $[n-r-h+r_a+1, \ldots, n]$ respectively, for Group $\perp$, Group 2, and Group 1. $h > 0$ and $r_a \geq 0$. If $-h + r_a \leq 0$, Group 2 of (j') consists entirely of principal components that belong to Group $\perp$ of the DGP. If $r_2 \geq -h+r_a > 0$, Group 2 of (j') has, in addition, (a portion of) those that are in Group 2 of the DGP. If $-h+r_a > r_2$, Group 2 of (j') has, further in addition, (a portion of) those in Group 1 of the DGP. (i) In general, unit root(s) may be rejected or accepted on Group 2 of (j'). If the unit root(s) is (are) rejected, the grouping method, (j'), is necessarily rejected. (ii) If the unit root(s) is (are) accepted, we move on to the trend test by TRT in (6.2) applied to Group 2 of (j'). The present situation has been investigated in (i) of Section 6.8.1. Admittedly the analysis there was made in terms of unconditional distributions of X_S, but here the analysis should be made in terms of the distribution conditional on that the unit root(s) has(have) been accepted on Group 2 of (j'). This difference in no way affects the proof of Proposition 6.7(ii). As indicated in its proof in Appendix A, the proof depends only on the difference in orders between the deterministic trend and other stochastic parts, and the orders in probability (as $T \to \infty$) of the stochastic parts are not increased by considering the orders in terms of the conditional distributions. By virtue of Proposition 6.7(ii), absence of trend in Group 2 of (j') is rejected in probability 1 if T is sufficiently large. Combining (i) and (ii) above we see that the grouping method, (j'), is rejected in probability 1 if T is large. QED

Let us assume the situation in (b) above, and suppose that we are interested in the probability in which the unit root(s) is (are) rejected on Group 2 of (j'), i.e., (j') is rejected at stage (i) above, before moving to stage (ii). We have to distinguish three cases, $-h + r_a \leq 0$, $r_2 \leq -h + r_a$, and $0 < -h + r_a < r_2$. (a) Consider the case where $-h+r_a \leq 0$ so that Group 2 of (j') consists of principal components in Group $\perp$ of the DGP. The result of the unit root test depends on whether

$$B_\perp \eta_{\perp,n-r-h+1}, \ldots, B_\perp \eta_{\perp,n-r-h+r_a}$$

belong to the cointegration space or not. If any one of them does, the unit root(s) is (are) rejected in probability 1 if T is large. If none of them does, the unit root(s) is (are) accepted in probability $1 - \alpha$, i.e., rejected in probability α. See (i) of Section 5.7.2. (b) Consider the case where $r_2 \leq -h + r_a$ so that the entire principal components of Group 2 of the DGP are included in Group 2 of (j'). The case where $r_2 = 0$ (so that Group 2 of the DGP is null) is included here. If at least one of $B_\perp \eta_{\perp,n-r-h+1}, \ldots, B_\perp \eta_{\perp,n-r}$ belongs to the cointegration space, the unit root is rejected in probability 1. Moreover, if $r_2 < -h + r_a$, so that some of the principal components of Group 1 of (j) are included in addition in Group 2 of (j'), the unit root is rejected in probability 1. It is when $r_2 = -h + r_a$ and none of $B_\perp \eta_{\perp,n-r-h+1}, \ldots, B_\perp \eta_{\perp,n-r}$ belongs to the cointegration space that the unit roots are accepted in probability, $1 - \alpha$, i.e., rejected in probability, α. See Proposition 5.8. (c) Finally consider the case where $0 < -h + r_a < r_2$, so that a subset (rather than a full set) of the components of Group 2 of the DGP is in Group 2 of (j'). It is difficult to specify the probability that the unit root(s) in Group 2 of (j') is (are) rejected. See (ii) of Section 5.7.1.

7.5 Supplement

Continuing with the supposition that the grouping method, (j), represents the DGP, let us consider the results of tests on the grouping methods, $(j+1), \ldots, (jmax)$. It will be seen that different pairs, (j) and (j'), where $j' > j$, produce a variety of different asymptotic results of tests, such as rejection in probability 1, rejection in probability $1 - \alpha$, rejection in probability less than $1 - \alpha$, and theoretically indeterminable probability of rejection. The case where $n = 3$ and $p = 2$ will be considered for concreteness. Table 7.2 has shown all the grouping methods that are consistent with the theoretical analyses in Chapters 2 and 3.

(a) Suppose that (j) is (1), representing the DGP. It will be seen that we cannot determine theoretically the probability of rejection of any one of (2), (3), (4), and (5) alternatively chosen as (j'). (i) Let $(j') = (2)$. $[2, 3]$ and "null" are, respectively, Group 2 and Group 1 in the DGP, while [2] and [3] are, respectively, Group 2 and Group 1 in the mistaken constituents of (2). In testing (2), $UURT$ is calculated on [2] and [3] separately, though they jointly belong to Group 2 of the DGP. The present situation has been investigated in (ii) of Section 5.7.1. The limit distribution of $UURT$ on either [2] or [3] is not known. We cannot determine the probability that (2) is rejected. (ii) Let $(j') = (3)$. "null" and $[2, 3]$ are Group 2 and Group 1 in the mistaken constituents of (3). $UURT$ is calculated on [2] and [3] separately though

[2, 3] belongs to Group 2 of the DGP. The limit distribution of $UURT$ is not known, and we cannot determine the probability that (3) is rejected. (iii) Let $(j') = (4)$. [1, 2] and [3] are respectively Group ⊥ and Group 2 in the mistaken constituents. Probabilities that unit roots are found in [2] or [3] on the basis of $UURT$ are not known. (If a unit root is not found in [3], (4) would be rejected, but we do not know its probability.) Consider the case where both [2] and [3] are judged to have a unit root. We apply the trend test, (6.2), to [2] and [3] separately. Although $n - r = 1$ in the DGP, it is mistaken as 2. The critical value applied to both [2] and [3] is $\hat{C}_{(2)}(\alpha, 1)$, which is obtained by substituting $\hat{Q}_{(2)}$ for Q in (6.6). The test on [3] has been analysed in (i) of Section 6.8.2. The probability that TRT exceeds $\hat{C}_{(2)}(\alpha, 1)$ cannot be specified. The test on [2] has been analysed in (ii) of Section 6.8.2 (on the case where $r_2 > 1$). The probability that TRT exceeds $\hat{C}_{(2)}(\alpha, 1)$ is not known. We cannot determine the probability that (4) is rejected. (iv) Let $(j') = (5)$. [1, 2], "null", [3] are Group ⊥, Group 2, and Group 1 in the mistaken constituents. $UURT$ is calculated on [2] and [3] separately, but the limit distribution is not known. Suppose that a unit root is found in [2]. TRT with $d = 1$ is calculated on [2], and compared with $\hat{C}_{(2)}(\alpha, 1)$. The present situation has been investigated in (ii) of Section 6.8.2. We cannot determine the probability that (5) is rejected.

(b) Suppose that (j) is (2), representing the DGP. (i) Let $(j') = (3)$. [2] and [3] are, respectively, Group 2 and Group 1 in the DGP, while "null" and [2, 3] are Group 2 and Group 1 in mistaken constituents in (3). $UURT$ is calculated on [2] and [3] separately. Concerning [2], presence of the unit root is accepted in probability $1-\alpha$, which leads to rejection of (3). (3) is rejected in probability $1 - \alpha$. (ii) Let $(j') = (4)$. [1], [2], [3] are, respectively, Group ⊥, Group 2, and Group 1 in the DGP, and [1, 2], [3], and "null" are, respectively, Group ⊥, Group 2, and Group 1 in mistaken constituents in (4). $UURT$ is calculated on [2] and [3] separately. Presence of the unit root is rejected on [3], which leads to rejection of (4) in probability 1. This is sufficient for the analysis of grouping method (4) but let us investigate the remaining test of (4). The unit root should be found in [2] in probability $1-\alpha$. If it is, TRT with $d = 1$ is calculated on [2]. $n - r$ is 1 in the DGP, but it is mistaken as 2. If $\hat{C}_{(1)}(\alpha, 1)$ were used for the critical value of the TRT, presence of trend would be accepted only in probability α. But in fact $\hat{C}_{(2)}(\alpha, 1)$ is used, and $\hat{C}_{(2)}(\alpha, 1) < \hat{C}_{(1)}(\alpha, 1)$ by virtue of Lemma 6.4. Presence of trend is accepted in probability larger than α, which leads to rejection of (4) in probability less than $1 - \alpha$. (iii) Let $(j') = (5)$. [1] and [2] are Group ⊥ and Group 2, respectively, in the DGP, while [1,2] and "null" are Group ⊥ and Group 2 in mistaken constituents in (5). $UURT$ is calculated on

[2] and [3] separately. The previous result on [2] in (ii) above can be transferred to the present analysis. Presence of trend in [2] is accepted in probability larger than α, and the grouping method, (5), is rejected in probability less than $1 - \alpha$.

(c) Suppose that (j) is (3), representing the DGP. (i) Let (j') = (4). [1], "null", and [2, 3] are, respectively, Group $\perp$, Group 2, and Group 1 in the DGP, while [1, 2], [3], and "null" are Group $\perp$, Group 2, and Group 1 in mistaken constituents in (4). $UURT$ is calculated on [2] and [3] separately. It should diverge on [3], which leads to rejection of (4) in probability 1. This is sufficient for the consideration of the present case, but let us consider the remaining part of the test. Unit root is rejected on [2] in probability 1 because it in fact belongs to Group 1. The trend test is based on (6.1), and the trend should be rejected in probability 1. Thus (4) is rejected in probability 1 on this regard as well. (ii) (j') = (5). [1] and [2, 3] are, respectively, Group $\perp$ and Group 1 in the DGP, and [1, 2] and [3] are Group $\perp$ and Group 1 in a mistaken constituent, (5). The result on [2] given in (i) above can be transferred here. (5) is rejected in probability 1.

(d) Suppose that (j) is (4), representing the DGP, while (j') = (5). [3] and "null" are, respectively, Group 2 and Group 1 in the DGP, while "null" and [3] are, respectively, Group 2 and Group 1 in mistaken constituents in (5). Absence of unit root in [3] is accepted only in probability α because it in fact belongs to Group 2. (5) is rejected in probability $1 - \alpha$.

The above (b), (c), and (d) may be summarised as follows. Concerning the combinations of (j) and (j') such that $j' > j > 1$, we can determine the asymptotic probabilities of rejecting (j'). They are equal to either 1 or $1 - \alpha$ except for one combination, (j) = (2) and (j') = (5), where the probability is less than $1 - \alpha$.

8 Simulation Studies

In the previous chapters all the reasoning has proceeded on the asymptotic theories, while the methods derived there anticipate their applications to macroeconomic studies involving about 100 to 200 quarterly observations. The present chapter presents our simulation studies for the case where $n = 2$, $p = 2$, $T = 100$ or 200, and $SH = [\boldsymbol{t}, \boldsymbol{dt}(b)]$ with $b = 0.5$. Section 8.1 will describe seven DGPs that incorporate a variety of structures of deterministic trends as well as different cointegration structures. Section 8.2 will give a detailed description of the trend test for I(0) for the special case of n, p, and SH, because the test was only outlined in Section 6.1 for the general case. Section 8.3 will begin with the reiteration of the asymptotic reasoning on the special case of n, p, and SH, which leads to a table of probabilities, Table 8.4, which we should expect if we had an infinite sample size. The table is arranged so that it can be easily compared with the tables of probabilities produced by simulations on finite sample sizes. In Section 8.3 we shall also give instruction on the last grouping method, which was left unclear in Chapter 7. Section 8.4 will present our simulations studies. The design of simulations incorporates data-dependence of the critical values of the trend test for I(1). Some discrepancies are discovered between the asymptotic theory and the simulation results with $T = 100$ and 200, and the discrepancies are analysed. Section 8.5 will present an example of applications to Japanese macroeconomic time series.

8.1 DGP

We shall simulate models in the form,

$$x_t = d_t + s_t,$$

$$\Delta d_t = FB' d_{t-1} + M(\phi) h_{T,t},$$

$$\Delta s_t = \alpha\beta' s_{t-1} + u_t.$$

x_t, d_t, s_t, and u_t are each 2×1. u_t is a sequence of white noise with zero mean vector and covariance matrix, $\sigma^2 I_2$. When T is 100 (200), $h_{T,t}$ is $[1, 0]'$ for $t \leq 50$ (100), and $[1, 1]'$ for $t \geq 51$ (101). F and B are each $2 \times r$, $r = 0, 1$, and chosen so that $\text{rank}(F) = \text{rank}(B) = r$ and $I_r + B'F$ is stable. $M(\phi)$ has the role of M in the equation (2.5) in Chapter 2, and

$$M(\phi) = \begin{bmatrix} 1 & 0 \\ 1 & \phi \end{bmatrix}.$$

SH_TM' in Chapter 2 is here $[\boldsymbol{t}, \boldsymbol{t} + \phi \boldsymbol{dt}(0.5)]$. Unless $\phi = 0$ the second column represents a trend with a break at the midpoint of the sample period. If $\phi < 0$ the slope in the second sub-period is less than that in the first.

Seven sets of values of F, B, α, and β are listed in Table 8.1. Each set will be combined with $\phi = -0.5, 0.5$. In the DGPs 1, 2, 3, and 4,

$$F_{\perp}(B_{\perp}' F_{\perp})^{-1} B_{\perp} = [0, 1]'[0.5, 1]$$

so that

$$X_{D\perp} = (\boldsymbol{t} + \phi \boldsymbol{dt}(0.5))[0.5, 1]$$

by virtue of (2.9). The trends in the first and the second variables are identical except for their coefficients, 0.5 and 1, respectively. The trend that is common is $\boldsymbol{t} + \phi \boldsymbol{dt}(0.5)$. In the DGPs 5, 6, and 7, we may regard that neither F nor B exists; what is important is that $F_{\perp} = B_{\perp} = I_2$. Thus,

$$X_{D\perp} = [\boldsymbol{t}, \boldsymbol{t} + \phi \boldsymbol{dt}(0.5)].$$

The first variable has a linear trend, while the second variable has a trend with a kink.

The last four columns of Table 8.1 will be explained. We have described in Section 3.1 how Group $\perp$, Group 2, and Group 1 are formed. They involve, respectively, $n-r$, r_2, and r_1 principal components in the descending order of eigenvalues. $n-r$ is the number of the deterministic common trends. r_2 is the number of co-trending relations that are not a cointegration relation. r_1 is the number of co-trending relations that are also a cointegration relation. When $r = 1$ as in the DGPs 1 through 4, B represents the co-trending relation. There is one common deterministic trend so that $n - r = 1$. When $r = 0$ as in the DGPs, 5, 6, 7, there is no co-trending relation. Two common deterministic trends are involved so that $n-r$ is 2. In the DGP 1 there is no cointegration in s_t so that the co-trending relation cannot be a cointegration relation. Therefore, $r_2 = 1$ and $r_1 = 0$. In the DGP 2 there is one cointegration relation, β, but

Table 8.1. Parameters of the DGP

DGP	F'	B'	α'	β'	$n-r$	r_2	r_1	Grouping method
1	$[1,0]$	$[-1,0.5]$	0_2	0_2	1	1	0	(1)
2	$[1,0]$	$[-1,0.5]$	$[-1,0.5]$	$[1,0.5]$	1	1	0	(1)
3	$[1,0]$	$[-1,0.5]$	$-0.5I_2$	I_2	1	0	1	(2)
4	$[1,0]$	$[-1,0.5]$	$[1,0]$	$[-1,0.5]$	1	0	1	(2)
5	-	-	0_2	0_2	2	0	0	(3)
6	-	-	$[1,0]$	$[-1,0.5]$	2	0	0	(3)
7	-	-	$-0.5I_2$	I_2	2	0	0	(3)

Note: 0_2 and I_2 are 2×2 zero and unit matrices respectively.

Table 8.2. Grouping methods in the case of $n = 2$, $p = 2$

Grouping method (1) :	Group $\perp = [1]$	Group 2 = [2]	Group 1 = "null"
Grouping method (2) :	Group $\perp = [1]$	Group 2 = "null"	Group 1 = [2]
Grouping method (3) :	Group $\perp = [1,2]$	Group 2 = "null"	Group 1 = "null"

it is different from the co-trending relation, B. Therefore, $r_2 = 1$ and $r_1 = 0$. In the DGP 3 s_t is I(0), and any vectors can be a cointegration vector. Thus the co-trending relation, B, is also a cointegration relation. Therefore, $r_2 = 0$ and $r_1 = 1$. In the DGP 4 there is one co-trending relation, B, and one cointegration relation, β. Moreover $B = \beta$. Therefore, $r_2 = 0$ and $r_1 = 1$. In the DGPs 5, 6, 7, $r = 0 = r_1 + r_2$ and $r_2 = r_1 = 0$.

With $n - r$, r_2, and r_1 we can determine the constituents of Group $\perp$, Group 2, and Group 1, i.e., a grouping method is selected. In Chapter 7 we have explained how to order all the grouping methods that are consistent with the theory developed in Chapter 3. They are presented in Table 8.2 on the special case of $n = 2$, $p = 2$. Each of the seven DGPs listed in Table 8.1 is assigned to one and only one of the grouping methods in terms of $n - r$, r_2, and r_1. The grouping method in each DGP is indicated in Table 8.1.

The initials for d_t and s_t are respectively $d_0 = 0$ and $s_{-99} = 0$. σ^2 is chosen so that, given the other parameters, F, B, ϕ, α, β, each of the two variables of x_t has its signal-noise ratio in a range that is realistic as a macroeconomic time series. The signal noise ratio for the j-th ($j = 1, 2$) variable is defined as $d_j(T)/s_j(T)$, where

$$d_j(T) = \sum_{t=1}^{T} d_{tj}^2 - T^{-1}(\sum_{t=1}^{T} d_{tj})^2$$

$$s_j(T) = \mathrm{E}(\sum_{t=1}^{T} s_{tj}^2 - T^{-1}(\sum_{t=1}^{T} s_{tj})^2).$$

We have tried to choose σ^2 in each DGP so that the ratios for both variables are approximately between 50 and 200 for $T = 200$ and $\phi = -0.5$. We have been successful except for the first variable of the DGP 6, on which the ratio is 400.

8.2 Details of the Trend Test for I(0)

In Section 6.1 we have only outlined the trend test to be applied to the principal component that has been judged I(0). More details are given here for the case where SH is $[\boldsymbol{t}, \boldsymbol{dt}(b)]$, where $1 > b > 0$. Let $[x_1, \ldots, x_T]$ be the principal component to be investigated. The sample period is divided into $1, \ldots, [Tb]$ and $[Tb] + 1, \ldots, T$. The rate of increase in the sum of squares is investigated in each of the two sub-periods separately. Let a be a real number such that $3 > a > 1$. Construct

$$g_1 = z_1' z_1 / [Tb]^a - w_1' w_1 / m^a \tag{8.1}$$

and

$$g_2 = z_2' z_2 / (T - [Tb])^a - w_2' w_2 / m^a, \tag{8.2}$$

where

$$z_1' = [x_1 - x_1, \ldots, x_{[Tb]} - x_1], \quad z_2' = [x_{[Tb]+1} - x_{[Tb]+1}, \ldots, x_T - x_{[Tb]+1}],$$
$$w_1' = [x_1 - x_1, \ldots, x_m - x_1], \quad w_2' = [x_{[Tb]+1} - x_{[Tb]+1}, \ldots, x_{[Tb]+m} - x_{[Tb]+1}].$$

If either $g_1 > 0$ or $g_2 > 0$, we judge that x has a trend. If $g_1 \leq 0$ and $g_2 \leq 0$, x does not have a trend. If in fact x is I(0) and has no trend, g_1 and g_2 converge to negative values, $-w_1' w_1 / m^a$ and $-w_2' w_2 / m^a$, respectively, as $T \to \infty$. If x has a trend, both g_1 and g_2 diverge to ∞. In the simulation studies we have set $m = 20$ and $a = 2$.

8.3 A Table of Asymptotic Probabilities

8.3.1 Statistical Decision

Pretending ignorance of the DGP, we shall attempt to choose one of the three grouping methods in Table 8.2 as the one that fits the data best. This choice leads to determination of $n - r$, r_2, and r_1, i.e., r, r_2, and r_1. Following the sequential decision

Table 8.3. Outcomes of statistical decision

I(1) and trend-less	:	The grouping method (1) is our final choice
I(0) and trend-less	:	The grouping method (2) is our final choice
I(1) and trend	:	Move to testing the grouping method (3)
I(0) and trend	:	Move to testing the grouping method (3)

rule we test initially the grouping method (1). If it is accepted it is our final choice. If it is rejected we move to testing the grouping method (2). If it is accepted the grouping method (2) is our final choice. If it is rejected we move to testing of the grouping method (3). Let us stop here before implementing this test and collect all possible results of the tests so far involved. This is because we have not explicitly indicated what to do with the last grouping method in Chapter 7. Since $n = 2$ in our simulation studies, and since the first principal component is never investigated (see Section 7.3), the statistical properties of only the second principal component are used to discriminate different grouping methods in Table 8.2. The properties used are related to whether the component is I(0) or I(1) and whether it has a trend or not. Outcomes of our decision are listed in Table 8.3 on the basis of different combinations of the properties. The test of trend when the second principal component is judged I(0) uses (8.1) and (8.2). The test when it is I(1) uses (6.2) with $d = 1$. The null distribution is (6.3) with $\hat{Q}_{(1)}$ substituted for Q in (6.6), because $n - r = 1$ in the grouping methods 1 and 2.

8.3.2 Asymptotic Probabilities of Different Outcomes of the Decision

The above statistical decision can be analysed by the asymptotic theory applied to the knowledge about the DGP. In particular, asymptotic probabilities of different outcomes of the decision can be derived. They are shown in Table 8.4. The outcomes in the second column, I(1), and the third column, trend-less, together lead to the final choice of the grouping method (1). The outcomes of the fourth column, I(0), and the fifth column, trend-less, together lead to the final choice of the grouping method (2). α is the significance level in both the unit root test and the trend test for I(1).

The probabilities in Table 8.4 will be explained. When the DGP 1 generates the data, the second principal component belongs to Group 2. The theories in Chapters 5 and 6 show that the unit root is accepted in probability $1-\alpha$ asymptotically, and that absence of trend is accepted also in probability $1-\alpha$ asymptotically in the trend test for I(1). These are entered in the second and the third columns. The two tests are not

Table 8.4. Asymptotic probabilities of different outcomes

	Choosing grouping method (1)		Choosing grouping method (2)	
DGP	I(1)	Trend-less	I(0)	Trend-less
1, 2	$1-\alpha$	$1-\alpha$	α	?
3, 4	0	?	1	1
5, 6	$1-\alpha$	0	α	0
7	0	0	1	0

mutually independent, and the probability in the third column is not the probability conditional upon the acceptance of I(1). However, since the probability of the event that *either* I(1) is rejected *or* the trend-less is rejected is smaller than 2α by virtue of Bonferroni inequality, the probability of choosing the grouping method (1) is larger than $1 - 2\alpha$. Even though the principal component here is in fact a trend-less I(1) variable, the trend test for I(0) is performed with $a = 2$ in (8.1) and (8.2). We cannot determine the probability that the trend-less is accepted. We can only say that the grouping method (2) is chosen in probability less than α. These results imply that we move to testing the grouping method (3) in probability less than 2α. Recall that the DGP 1 belongs to the grouping method (1). The above reasoning is applicable to the case where the data is generated by the DGP 2, because the second principal component of this DGP also belongs to Group 2.

Suppose that the DGP 3 generates the data. The second principal component belongs to Group 1, and the unit root test statistic diverges to ∞ as $T \to \infty$. I(1) is accepted only in probability zero. Although we do not know the probability that the trend-less is accepted in the test for I(1), it does not prevent us from concluding that the grouping method (1) is chosen only with zero probability. On the other hand the trend-less is accepted in the test for I(0) with probability 1. The grouping method (2) is chosen in probability 1. The above reasoning is applicable to the DGP 4 as well. Recall that the DGPs 3 and 4 belong to the grouping method (2).

For the examination of the DGPs 5, 6, and 7 we note a result in Sections 5.2 and 5.3 that when the principal component belongs to Group $\perp$, the unit root is accepted in probability $1-\alpha$ if $B_{\perp}\eta_{\perp,2}$ is not a cointegration vector, and the unit root is rejected in probability 1 if $B_{\perp}\eta_{\perp,2}$ is a cointegration vector. When the data is generated by the DGP 5, the second principal component belongs to Group $\perp$. Since the stochastic part of the DGP 5 has no cointegration, $B_{\perp}\eta_{\perp,2}$ cannot be a cointegration vector. I(1) and I(0) are accepted in probabilities $1-\alpha$ and α, respectively. The trend test statistic for I(1) diverges to ∞ as $T \to \infty$. The trend test for I(0) is a misapplication to an I(1) variable with a trend, but $a = 2$ in (8.1) and (8.2) makes these statistics diverge. The trend-less is accepted only in probability zero. There is only zero probability for accepting either the grouping method (1) or (2), which means that we move to testing the grouping method (3) in probability 1.

Next we shall consider the DGP 7. Since the stochastic part of this DGP is I(0), any vector can be a cointegration vector. Thus $B_\perp \eta_{\perp,2}$ is a cointegration vector. The unit root test statistic diverges. I(1) and I(0) are accepted in probabilities 0 and 1, respectively. Proposition 6.3 shows that the trend test statistic for I(1) diverges, and the trend-less is accepted only in probability zero. So is the trend-less in the test for I(0). We move to testing the grouping method (3) in probability 1.

Finally the DGP 6 will be considered. The stochastic part is I(1) but cointegrated with the vector, $\beta = [-1, 0.5]'$. As for the deterministic part let us examine $B_\perp \eta_{\perp,2}$. $B_\perp$ may be regarded I_2 in the present DGP. Also

$$X_D = X_{D\perp} = (I - \boldsymbol{P}(\iota))SHM'(\phi).$$

$\eta_{\perp,2}$ is the eigenvector that corresponds to the second eigenvalue of

$$\lim_{T\to\infty} T^{-3} M(\phi)H'S'(I - \boldsymbol{P}(\iota))SHM'(\phi). \tag{8.3}$$

When $SH = [\boldsymbol{t}, \boldsymbol{dt}(b)]$, (8.3) is

$$M(\phi)\begin{bmatrix} 1/12 & 1/12 - b^2/4 + b^3/6 \\ 1/12 - b^2/4 + b^3/6 & (1/3)(1-b)^3 - (1/4)(1-b)^4 \end{bmatrix} M'(\phi).$$

With $b = 0.5$, $\phi = -0.5$, $B_\perp \eta_{\perp,2}$ is $[-1, 1.320]$, and with $b = 0.5$, $\phi = 0.5$ it is $[-1, 0.795]$. Both differ from β though the one with $\phi = 0.5$ is closer to β than the one with $\phi = -0.5$. In terms of the asymptotic theory, I(1) and I(0) are accepted in probabilities $1 - \alpha$ and α, respectively, and the trend-less is accepted in probability 0. We move to testing the grouping method (3) in probability 1.

8.3.3 Grouping Method (3)

Let us consider tests of the grouping method (3). It is accepted when the trend-less is rejected either in the test for I(1) or in the test for I(0). We can prove the following statement which holds on any DGP even with a finite T.

Proposition 8.1 *In regard to Table 8.2, suppose that the grouping methods (1) and (2) both have been rejected. Then the grouping method (3) is accepted if it is tested.*

Proof. Consider first the case where the second principal component is judged I(0). The trend test for I(0) must have rejected the trend-less, because the grouping method (2) has been rejected. This test is also a portion of the tests of the grouping method (3). Consider next the case where the second principal component is judged I(1). The trend test must have used $\hat{Q}_{(1)}$ for Q in (6.6) in deriving the critical value. This is not the trend test to be used for the grouping method (3). Here $\hat{Q}_{(2)}$ should be used because $n - r = 2$ in the grouping method (3). Lemma 6.4 shows that, given the same data, the critical value with $\hat{Q}_{(1)}$ is larger than the critical value with $\hat{Q}_{(2)}$. The fact that the grouping method (1) has been rejected means that the test statistic (6.2) exceeded the critical value with $\hat{Q}_{(1)}$. Thus the test statistic also exceeds the critical value with $\hat{Q}_{(2)}$, i.e., the trend-less is rejected in testing the grouping method (3). QED

Acceptance of the grouping method (3) as a consequence of rejecting the grouping methods (1) and (2) may be called passive acceptance. On the other hand, acceptance of the grouping method (3) through testing it with $\hat{Q}_{(2)}$ may be called positive acceptance. Proposition 8.1 states that if the grouping method (3) is passively accepted it must also be positively accepted. However, the converse does not hold. The trend test statistic for I(1) may fall between the critical values with $\hat{Q}_{(1)}$ and with $\hat{Q}_{(2)}$. If it does, the trend-less is accepted in testing the grouping method (1), and our sequential decision rule orders to terminate the procedure, leaving the grouping method (3) unexamined. Yet the grouping method (3) would be accepted if it is positively tested. The grouping method (3) is accepted positively but not passively, if and only if the grouping methods (1) and (3) are both accepted on their own.

The asymptotic probability of passive acceptance of the grouping method (3) has been given above for each DGP. It is less than 2α in the DGPs 1 and 2, zero in the DGPs 3 and 4, and 1 in the DGPs 5, 6, and 7. The asymptotic probability of positive acceptance of the grouping method (3) is zero in the DGPs 3 and 4, and 1 in the DGPs 5, 6, and 7. In particular, with respect to the DGPs 5 and 6 the trend test statistic diverges to ∞ as $T \to \infty$, exceeding both of the two critical values. Thus in terms of the asymptotic theory there is no discrepancy between the passive and the positive acceptance of the grouping method (3) in the DGPs 3 through 7. In the DGPs 1 and 2, since the trend test for I(1) uses the critical value based on $\hat{Q}_{(2)}$ for testing the grouping method (3), the trend is accepted in some probability larger than it is accepted in testing the grouping method (1). In the DGPs 1 and 2 the probability of positive acceptance of the grouping method (3) is larger than its passive acceptance even in the asymptotic theory. Since the DGPs 1 and 2 in fact belong to the grouping method (1), the acceptance of the grouping method (3) (or setting up the new category, undecided) is undesirable. The conclusion that follows from the asymptotic analyses is that the grouping method (3) should be accepted *only when it is passively accepted.*

Proposition 8.1 can be extended to the general case of n and p. For instance in regard to Table 7.2 the statement can be proved by comparing the grouping methods (2), (3), and (5) there. The above conclusion on the treatment of the last grouping method also generalises.

8.4 Results of Simulation Studies

We are especially concerned with the power of tests among possible weaknesses of the asymptotic reasoning. The unit root test has been subjected to extensive simulation examinations, and the results have been far from excellent especially on its power. Many econometric methods of testing have been found inadequate in their power when applied to 100 or 200 observations. Moreover, we should not forget that the unit root and trend tests are applied in our investigation to a non-standard time series, which the principal component is.

Given a finite sample size, let $P0$ and $P1$ denote the probabilities of accepting I(0) and I(1), respectively, on the second principal component. Let $rf0$ be the probability of accepting the presence of trend conditional upon the component being judged I(0), and let $rf1$ denote the probability of accepting the presence of trend conditional upon the component being judged I(1). Following the rules given in Table 8.3, the probability of choosing the grouping method (1) is $P1 \times (1 - rf1)$, and the probability of choosing the grouping method (2) is $P0 \times (1 - rf0)$. The probability of passively accepting the grouping method (3) is $1 - P1 \times (1 - rf1) - P0 \times (1 - rf0) \equiv P1 \times rf1 + P0 \times rf0$. For each DGP consider a row vector,

$$[P1, 1 - rf1, P0, 1 - rf0]. \tag{8.4}$$

Each row of Table 8.4 is the asymptotic value of (8.4) except for that the probability of trend-less conditional upon the outcomes of the unit root test replaces the unconditional probability.

In deriving $P1$, $1 - rf1$, $P0$, $1 - rf0$ by simulations, the dependence of the critical value on data must be accounted for on the trend test for I(1). Suppose that a realisation of X is produced, and that the second principal component is judged

Table 8.5. Probabilities in simulation experiments, $T = 800$

					Grouping method		
DGP	$P1$	$1-rf1$	$P0$	$1-rf0$	(1)	(2)	(3)
1	0.940	0.950	0.060	0.485	0.893	0.029	0.078
2	0.939	0.955	0.061	0.537	0.896	0.033	0.071
3	0.000	–	1.000	1.000	0.000	1.000	0.000
4	0.000	–	1.000	1.000	0.000	1.000	0.000
5	0.943	0.000	0.057	0.000	0.000	0.000	1.000
6	0.913	0.000	0.087	0.000	0.000	0.000	1.000
7	0.000	–	1.000	0.001	0.000	0.001	0.999

Note: $\alpha = 0.05$, $b = 0.5$, $\phi = -0.5$, 5,000 iterations, $k = 5$

I(1). (i) Calculate the statistic, TRT, in (6.2) and the reduced rank regression of X on SH, $\hat{Q}_{(1)}$. (ii) The probability distribution of (6.3) is derived from a sufficiently large number of realisations of the demeaned, 1-dimensional Brownian motion, $\tilde{B}$, while fixing Q in (6.6) at $\hat{Q}_{(1)}$. The upper α point in this distribution is the critical point. (iii) The statistic, TRT, is compared with the critical value to judge presence or absence of trend. The procedure (ii) has to be re-executed every time a new realisation of X is produced such that the second principal component is judged I(1).

Our simulation results are presented in Tables 8.5 through 8.7. The entries headed by the title, $P1$, $1 - rf1$, $P0$, and $1 - rf0$ show (8.4) for each DGP. These portions of the tables are each comparable with Table 8.4. The entries headed by the title, grouping method, give probabilities of choosing the given grouping method. In particular, the choice of grouping method (3) means passive acceptance of this grouping. Experiments are based on 5,000 iterations. The piecewise linear trends are constructed with $\phi = -0.5$. The significance levels for the unit root test and the trend test for I(1) are both $\alpha = 0.05$. The lag order in the unit root test is $k = 5$. We reiterate that the statistical properties of only the second principal component are used to choose one from the grouping methods, (1), (2), and (3). The choice is made in the sequential order of (1) and (2), and (3) is chosen only when both (1) and (2) are rejected.

Table 8.5 for $T = 800$ is presented to confirm the validity of the asymptotic probabilities in Table 8.4. Indeed the probabilities in the two tables are found close

Table 8.6. Probabilities in simulation experiments, $T = 100$

DGP	$P1$	$1 - rf1$	$P0$	$1 - rf0$	Grouping method (1)	(2)	(3)
1	0.933	0.952	0.067	0.499	0.888	0.034	0.078
2	0.924	0.965	0.076	0.485	0.892	0.037	0.071
3	0.548*	1.000	0.452*	0.968	0.548	0.438	0.014
4	0.246*	1.000	0.754*	0.995	0.246	0.750	0.004
5	0.932	0.345*	0.068	0.071	0.321*	0.005	0.674
6	0.909	0.211*	0.091	0.011	0.192*	0.001	0.807
7	0.535*	1.000	0.465*	0.503*	0.535	0.234	0.231

Note: $\alpha = 0.05$, $b = 0.5$, $\phi = -0.5$, 5,000 iterations, $k = 5$

to each other. Table 8.6 for $T = 100$ reveals a number of problems in relation to the entries marked with $*$. (a) In the DGPs 3, 4, and 7 the second principal component is in fact I(0), and $P1$ should be much smaller (and $P0$ should be much larger) than indicated in the table. This defect reveals weakness of the power of the unit root test. (b) In the DGP 7 the second principal component is in fact I(0) with a trend, and $1 - rf0$ is the probability of judging it as trend-less. $1 - rf0$ for the DGP 7 should be much smaller than indicated in Table 8.6. The discriminatory power of the trend test for I(0) is found to be weak. (c) In the DGPs 5 and 6, $1 - rf1$ should be much smaller than the entries in the table. Since we are testing here the grouping method (1) on the second principal component, the critical value in the trend test for I(1) is based on $\hat{Q}_{(1)}$. If it were known that the DGP is either 5 or 6, we would apply the critical value based on $\hat{Q}_{(2)}$ because the DGP in either case is associated with the grouping method (3). When T is large this should not matter because the second principal component has a trend which makes the test statistic diverge. Large values of $1 - rf1$ in the table indicate weakness of the power of the trend test when T is small. The fact that the critical value based on $\hat{Q}_{(1)}$ exceeds that on $\hat{Q}_{(2)}$ worsens the results, giving unusually large probabilities of accepting the null hypothesis, trend-less. The present defect is related to the discrepancy between the positive and the passive acceptance of the grouping method, (3), in finite samples. Let us turn our attention to Table 8.7, where T is increased to 200. We see that all three defects

Table 8.7. Probabilities in simulation experiments, $T = 200$

					Grouping method		
DGP	$P1$	$1 - rf1$	$P0$	$1 - rf0$	(1)	(2)	(3)
1	0.940	0.954	0.060	0.546	0.897	0.033	0.070
2	0.939	0.955	0.061	0.563	0.897	0.034	0.069
3	0.016	1.000	0.984	0.998	0.016	0.982	0.002
4	0.000	–	1.000	1.000	0.000	1.000	0.000
5	0.941	0.086	0.059	0.003	0.081	0.000	0.919
6	0.917	0.011	0.083	0.002	0.010	0.000	0.990
7	0.014	0.986	0.986	0.181	0.014	0.178	0.808

Note: $\alpha = 0.05$, $b = 0.5$, $\phi = -0.5$, 5,000 iterations, $k = 5$

are substantially reduced, though the defect (b) still remains to some extent. We conclude that satisfactory performance of our method requires $T = 200$.

We have also investigated the case where the piecewise linear trend is constructed by $\phi = 0.5$. The results are by and large similar to those above. The only point worth reporting is concerned with the relation between $B_{\perp}\eta_{\perp,2}$ and β in the DGP 6, which was mentioned at the end of Section 8.3.2. When $\phi = 0.5$, $B_{\perp}\eta_{\perp,2}$ is closer to β. It is found that $P0$ in the DGP is larger than in the case of $\phi = -0.5$. However, the probabilities of choosing different grouping methods are not much affected.

8.5 Empirical Example

To illustrate the applicability of our methodology to economic time series, we apply it to determine both r and r_1 of two Japanese macroeconomic time series presented in Figure 1.2, that is, natural logarithm of quarterly, seasonally adjusted real GDP and nominal money supply (M2+CD) over the period from 1980(I) to 2001(III). We note that the number of observations is 87. As is easily observed from Figure 1.2, the break point of trends of these two time series is located about the same time; roughly speaking, the middle point of the sample period. Hence we set $b = 0.5$ in this examination. The level of significances and the values of parameters, a, m, and k were set equal to the same values in the previous simulation experiments.

As a result of this examination, grouping method (1) was chosen, which indicates that $r = 1$ and $r_1 = 0$. This means that these two time series have one co-trending relation, in other words, they contain one common deterministic trend characterised by the existence of a break at the middle point of sample period. The result additionally indicates that the co-trending relation is not a cointegrating relation.

A Mathematical Proofs

A.1 Mathematical Proofs of Propositions and Lemmas in Chapter 2

A.1.1 Proof of Proposition 2.1

Because of Lemma 2.1(ii) we have an identity,

$$F(B'F)^{-1}B' + B_\perp(F'_\perp B_\perp)^{-1}F'_\perp = I_n,$$

$$\text{i.e., } d_t = F(B'F)^{-1}B'd_t + B_\perp(F'_\perp B_\perp)^{-1}F'_\perp d_t. \tag{A.1}$$

From (2.5) in the text it follows that $d_t = (I_n + FB')d_{t-1} + Mh_{T,t}$ with $d_0 = 0$. Premultiplication by $F'_\perp$ yields

$$F'_\perp d_t = F'_\perp M \sum_{s=1}^{t} h_{T,s}, \tag{A.2}$$

and premultiplication by B' yields

$$B'd_t = \sum_{j=0}^{t-1}(I_r + B'F)^j B'Mh_{T,t-j}. \tag{A.3}$$

Proposition 2.1 follows from substitution of (A.2) and (A.3) into the RHS of (A.1).

A.2 Mathematical Proofs of Propositions and Lemmas in Chapter 3

Proofs of Propositions 3.1, 3.2, and 3.3 use definitions of $\hat{\lambda}_i$ and $\hat{\xi}_i$ by

$$(T^{-3}X'X - \hat{\lambda}_i I)\hat{\xi}_i = 0, \quad \| \hat{\xi}_i \| = 1, \quad i = 1, \ldots, n. \tag{A.4}$$

Assumption 2.1 and the construction of $B_\perp$, B_2, and B_1 are crucial in the proofs.

A.2.1 Proof of Proposition 3.1

A.2.1.1 Proof of Proposition 3.1(i)

Let $\lambda_i(\cdot)$ denote the i-th eigenvalue (in descending order) of the matrix in $(\cdot)$. Since $\boldsymbol{B}$ is orthogonal,

$$\hat{\lambda}_i \equiv \lambda_i(T^{-3}X'X) = \lambda_i(\boldsymbol{B}'T^{-3}X'X\boldsymbol{B}).$$

Since the eigenvalues are continuous functions of the matrix,

$$\text{plim}_{T\to\infty}\,\lambda_i(\boldsymbol{B}'T^{-3}X'X\boldsymbol{B}) = \lambda_i(\text{plim}_{T\to\infty}\,\boldsymbol{B}'T^{-3}X'X\boldsymbol{B}).$$

From Assumptions 2.1 and 3.1 and from the construction of $B_\perp$, B_2, and B_1, $X_D B_1$ and $X_D B_2$ are $O(T^{1/2})$, $X_D B_\perp \gamma$ is $O(T^{3/2})$ not $o(T^{3/2})$ for any γ, $X_S B_1$ is $O_p(T^{1/2})$, and $X_S B_2$ and $X_S B_\perp$ are $O_p(T)$. Elements of

$$\text{plim}_{T\to\infty}[B_\perp, B_2, B_1]'T^{-3}X'X[B_\perp, B_2, B_1]$$

are zero except one block, $\text{plim}_{T\to\infty}\,B'_\perp T^{-3}X'XB_\perp$. In the present proposition $i = 1,\ldots,n-r$, and

$$\lambda_i(\text{plim}_{T\to\infty}\,\boldsymbol{B}'T^{-3}X'X\boldsymbol{B}) = \lambda_i(\text{plim}_{T\to\infty}\,B'_\perp T^{-3}X'XB_\perp) = \lambda_i(G_{\perp\perp}) \equiv \lambda_i.$$

The remaining eigenvalues of $T^{-3}X'X$ converge in probability to zero.

A.2.1.2 Proof of Proposition 3.1(ii)

(ii) is implied in (iii).

A.2.1.3 Proof of Proposition 3.1(iii)

Define $\hat{\eta}_i$, $n \times 1$, $\| \hat{\eta}_i \| = 1$ by

$$\boldsymbol{B}'(T^{-3}X'X - \hat{\lambda}_i I)\boldsymbol{B}\hat{\eta}_i = 0, \tag{A.5}$$

$$\text{i.e., } (\boldsymbol{B}'T^{-3}X'X\boldsymbol{B} - \hat{\lambda}_i I)\hat{\eta}_i = 0. \tag{A.6}$$

Since $\boldsymbol{B}'$ is nonsingular, it follows from (A.4) and (A.5) that

$$\hat{\xi}_i = \boldsymbol{B}\hat{\eta}_i. \tag{A.7}$$

Decompose $\hat{\eta}_i = [\hat{\eta}'_{\perp,i}, \hat{\eta}'_{2,i}, \hat{\eta}'_{1,i}]'$. Here we consider $i = 1,\ldots,n-r$. In the limit (A.6) takes the form,

$$\text{diag}[G_{\perp\perp} - \lambda_i I_{n-r}, -\lambda_i I_{r_2}, -\lambda_i I_{r_1}][\eta'_{\perp,i}, \eta'_{2,i}, \eta'_{1,i}]' = [0', 0', 0']', \tag{A.8}$$

i.e., $\hat{\eta}_i$ converges to $\eta_i = [\eta'_{\perp,i}, \eta'_{2,i}, \eta'_{1,i}]'$. (A.8) implies that $\eta_{2,i} = 0$, $\eta_{1,i} = 0$, and $\eta_{\perp,i}$ is the eigenvector of $G_{\perp\perp}$ associated with λ_i. Compare (A.6) and (A.8). With Assumption 3.2(ii) the difference between $\boldsymbol{B}'T^{-3}X'X\boldsymbol{B}$ in (A.6) and $\mathrm{diag}[G_{\perp\perp}, 0, 0]$ in (A.8) is $O_p(T^{-1/2})$. Since $\hat{\lambda}_i$ and λ_i are the eigenvalues of the former and the latter, respectively, $\hat{\lambda}_i - \lambda_i$ is $O_p(T^{-1/2})$, which holds true even if $G_{\perp\perp}$ has eigenvalues in multiplicity. The difference between $-\hat{\lambda}_i I$ in (A.6) and $\mathrm{diag}[-\lambda_i I_{n-r}, -\lambda_i I_{r_2}, -\lambda_i I_{r_1}]$ in (A.8) is $O_p(T^{-1/2})$. Therefore, $\hat{\eta}_i - \eta_i$ is $O_p(T^{-1/2})$.(13) In particular, $\hat{\eta}_{2,i} = O_p(T^{-1/2})$, $\hat{\eta}_{1,i} = O_p(T^{-1/2})$, and $\hat{\eta}_{\perp,i} = \eta_{\perp,i} + O_p(T^{-1/2})$. Substitution of these results into (A.7) proves (iii) of the proposition including (3.2) on $\Gamma_{\perp\perp}$.

A.2.1.4 Proof of Proposition 3.1(iv)

$$\begin{aligned} T^{-3/2}X[\hat{\xi}_1, \ldots, \hat{\xi}_{n-r}] &= T^{-3/2}(X_D + X_S)(B_\perp \Gamma_{\perp\perp} + B_2\Gamma_{2\perp} + B_1\Gamma_{1\perp}) \\ &= T^{-3/2}X_D B_\perp[\eta_{\perp,1}, \ldots, \eta_{\perp,n-r}] + O_p(T^{-1/2}). \end{aligned}$$

A.2.2 Proof of Proposition 3.2

A.2.2.1 Proof of Proposition 3.2(i)

We shall use a method adopted in Johansen (1991) to reveal the eigenvalues, in $O_p(T^{-1})$, of the data covariance matrix, suppressing those in $O_p(1)$. Let $D_T = \mathrm{diag}[I_{n-r}, T^{1/2}I_{r_2}, T^{1/2}I_{r_1}]$. The roots of $\det[T^{-3}X'X - \lambda I] = 0$ are the roots of

$$\det[D_T \boldsymbol{B}'(T^{-3}X'X - \lambda I)\boldsymbol{B} D_T] = 0. \tag{A.9}$$

Construct $Z_1 = T^{-3}B'_\perp X'XB_\perp$, $Z_2 = T^{-2}[B_2, B_1]'X'X[B_2, B_1]$, and

$$Z_3 = T^{-5/2}B'_\perp X'X[B_2, B_1].$$

Then (A.9) is rewritten as

$$\det[Z_1 - \lambda I_{n-r}]\det[Z_2 - Z_3'(Z_1 - \lambda I_{n-r})^{-1}Z_3 - T\lambda I_r] = 0. \tag{A.10}$$

$r = r_2 + r_1$. While we let T go to infinity, we make $T\lambda$ be $O_p(1)$ so that λ is $O_p(T^{-1})$. The first determinant on the LHS of (A.10) cannot be zero when T is sufficiently large, implying that the second determinant must be zero. Concerning $Z_2 - Z_3'(Z_1 - \lambda I_{n-r})^{-1}Z_3$, all elements other than its first $r_2 \times r_2$ diagonal block converge to zero. It can also be seen that this $r_2 \times r_2$ block and (3.6) in the text are asymptotically identical, partly because λI_{n-r} is $O_p(T^{-1})$. Writing $T\lambda \xrightarrow{w} \lambda_*$, the second determinant in (A.10) being zero is asymptotically expressed as $\det[\mathrm{diag}[U_{22}, 0] - \lambda_* I_r] = 0$, where U_{22} is defined in (3.5) as the limiting expression of (3.6). $T\lambda$ weakly converges to $\lambda_1(U_{22}), \ldots, \lambda_{r_2}(U_{22})$ and zeroes in multiplicity, $(r - r_2)$. The eigenvalues of U_{22} are a.s. single. Among the eigenvalues of the data covariance matrix it is $\hat{\lambda}_{n-r+1}, \ldots, \hat{\lambda}_{n-r+r_2}$ that are $O_p(T^{-1})$ but not $o_p(T^{-1})$.

A.2.2.2 Proof of Proposition 3.2(iii)

Construct $\hat{\eta}_{n-r+i}$ for $i = 1, \ldots, r_2$ by

$$D_T \boldsymbol{B}'(T^{-3}X'X - \hat{\lambda}_{n-r+i}I)\boldsymbol{B}D_T\hat{\eta}_{n-r+i} = 0, \quad \| \hat{\eta}_{n-r+i} \| = 1. \tag{A.11}$$

Since $D_T\boldsymbol{B}'$ is nonsingular, it follows from (A.4) and (A.11) that

$$\hat{\xi}_{n-r+i} = \| \boldsymbol{B}D_T\hat{\eta}_{n-r+i} \|^{-1} \boldsymbol{B}D_T\hat{\eta}_{n-r+i}. \tag{A.12}$$

With the notation used in (3.4) in the text let

$$W(\lambda_i(U_{22})) = \begin{bmatrix} G_{\perp\perp} & W_{\perp 2} & 0 \\ W_{2\perp} & W_{22} - \lambda_i(U_{22})I_{r_2} & 0 \\ 0 & 0 & -\lambda_i(U_{22})I_{r_1} \end{bmatrix}$$

which is what $D_T\boldsymbol{B}'(T^{-3}X'X - \hat{\lambda}_{n-r+i}I)\boldsymbol{B}D_T$ converges to. We can confirm

$$W(\lambda_i(U_{22})) \| \zeta_i \|^{-1} \zeta_i = 0, \tag{A.13}$$

where $\zeta_i' = [[-G_{\perp\perp}^{-1}W_{\perp 2}\eta_{2,i}]', \eta_{2,i}', 0']$, and $\eta_{2,i}$ is the normalised eigenvector of U_{22} associated with $\lambda_i(U_{22})$. Using Assumption 3.3(ii) in the comparison between (A.11) for a finite T and (A.13) for the limit, we see in the same way as in the proof of (iii) of Proposition 3.1 that $\hat{\eta}_{n-r+i} - \| \zeta_i \|^{-1} \zeta_i$ is $O_p(T^{-1/2})$. To be more explicit, writing $\| \zeta_i \|^{-1} \eta_{2,i} = \eta_{2,i}^*$,

$$\hat{\eta}_{n-r+i} \equiv \begin{bmatrix} \hat{\eta}_{\perp,n-r+i} \\ \hat{\eta}_{2,n-r+i} \\ \hat{\eta}_{1,n-r+i} \end{bmatrix} = \begin{bmatrix} -G_{\perp\perp}^{-1}W_{\perp 2}\eta_{2,i}^* \\ \eta_{2,i}^* \\ 0 \end{bmatrix} + O_p(T^{-1/2}). \tag{A.14}$$

Part (iii) of the proposition, including (3.7) and (3.8), is proved by substitution of (A.14) into (A.12), while noting that $\| \boldsymbol{B}D_T\hat{\eta}_{n-r+i} \|^{-1} = T^{-1/2} \| \eta_{2,i}^* \|^{-1} + O_p(T^{-1})$, and $\| \eta_{2,i}^* \|^{-1} \eta_{2,i}^* = \eta_{2,i}$.

A.2.2.3 Proof of Proposition 3.2(iv)

$$\begin{aligned} & T^{-1}X[\hat{\xi}_{n-r+1}, \ldots, \hat{\xi}_{n-r+r_2}] \\ =& T^{-1}(X_S + X_D)(B_\perp \Gamma_{\perp 2} + B_2\Gamma_{22} + B_1\Gamma_{12}) \\ =& (T^{-1}X_S B_2 - T^{-3/2}X_D B_\perp G_{\perp\perp}^{-1}W_{\perp 2})[\eta_{2,1}, \ldots, \eta_{2,r_2}] + O_p(T^{-1/2}) \\ =& T^{-1}(I - \boldsymbol{P}(X_D B_\perp))X_S B_2[\eta_{2,1}, \ldots, \eta_{2,r_2}] + O_p(T^{-1/2}), \end{aligned}$$

where

$$G_{\perp\perp}^{-1}W_{\perp 2} = (T^{-3}B_\perp' X_D' X_D B_\perp)^{-1}(T^{-5/2}B_\perp' X_D' X_S B_2) + O_p(T^{-1/2}) \tag{A.15}$$

has been used.

A.2.3 Proof of Proposition 3.3

The proof is analogous to that of Proposition 3.2. We shall indicate some salient points only.

A.2.3.1 Proof of Proposition 3.3(i)

$D_T = [I_{n-r}, T^{1/2}I_{r_2}, TI_{r_1}]$. $T^2\lambda$ is $O_p(1)$. When T is large, $\det[D_T\boldsymbol{B}'(T^{-3}X'X - \lambda I)\boldsymbol{B}D_T] = 0$ necessitates $\det[Z_1 - Z_2'Z_3^{-1}Z_2 - T^2\lambda I_{r_1}] = 0$, where $Z_1 = T^{-1}B_1'X'XB_1$, $Z_2 = [T^{-3/2}XB_\perp, T^{-1}XB_2]'T^{-1/2}XB_1$, and

$$Z_3 = [T^{-3/2}XB_\perp, T^{-1}XB_2]'[T^{-3/2}XB_\perp, T^{-1}XB_2].$$

$Z_1 - Z_2'Z_3^{-1}Z_2$ is (3.12) in the text, and weakly converges to U_{11} in (3.11).

A.2.3.2 Proof of Proposition 3.3(iii)

Construct $\hat{\eta}_{n-r_1+i}$ for $i = 1, \ldots, r_1$ by

$$D_T\boldsymbol{B}'(T^{-3}X'X - \hat{\lambda}_{n-r_1+i}I)\boldsymbol{B}D_T\hat{\eta}_{n-r_1+i} = 0; \| \hat{\eta}_{n-r_1+i} \| = 1. \tag{A.16}$$

With (A.4) we obtain $\hat{\xi}_{n-r_1+i} = \| \boldsymbol{B}D_T\hat{\eta}_{n-r_1+i} \|^{-1} \boldsymbol{B}D_T\hat{\eta}_{n-r_1+i}$. Let $W^{(1)}$, F_{11}, $A_\perp$, and A_2 be as defined in the text between (3.10) and (3.13). (A.16) weakly converges to $(W^{(1)} + \mathrm{diag}[0,0,F_{11}] - \lambda(U_{11})\,\mathrm{diag}[0,0,I_{r_1}]) \| \zeta_i \|^{-1} \zeta_i = 0$, where

$$\zeta_i = \begin{bmatrix} -A_\perp[G_{1\perp}, W_{12}]'\eta_{1,i} \\ -A_2[G_{1\perp}, W_{12}]'\eta_{1,i} \\ \eta_{1,i} \end{bmatrix}$$

with $\eta_{1,i}$ as the eigenvector of U_{11}. Writing $\| \zeta_i \|^{-1} \eta_{1,i} = \eta^*_{1,i}$,

$$\hat{\eta}_{n-r_1+i} = \begin{bmatrix} \hat{\eta}_{\perp,n-r_1+i} \\ \hat{\eta}_{2,n-r_1+i} \\ \hat{\eta}_{1,n-r_1+i} \end{bmatrix} = \begin{bmatrix} -A_\perp[G_{1\perp}, W_{12}]'\eta^*_{1,i} \\ -A_2[G_{1\perp}, W_{12}]'\eta^*_{1,i} \\ \eta^*_{1,i} \end{bmatrix} + O_p(T^{-1/2}). \tag{A.17}$$

Substitute (A.17) into (A.16).

A.2.3.3 Proof of Proposition 3.3(iv)

$$\begin{aligned}
&T^{-1/2}X[\hat{\xi}_{n-r_1+1}, \ldots, \hat{\xi}_n] \\
=&T^{-1/2}(X_D + X_S)(B_\perp\Gamma_{\perp 1} + B_2\Gamma_{21} + B_1\Gamma_{11}) \\
=&T^{-1/2}XB_1[\eta_{1,1}, \ldots, \eta_{1,r_1}] + T^{-1/2}[X_DB_\perp, X_SB_2][\Gamma_{\perp 1}', \Gamma_{21}']' + O_p(T^{-1/2}) \\
=&(T^{-1/2}XB_1 - [T^{-3/2}X_DB_\perp, T^{-1}X_SB_2][A_\perp', A_2']'[G_{1\perp}, W_{12}]')[\eta_{1,1}, \ldots, \eta_{1,r_1}] \\
&\quad + O_p(T^{-1/2}) \\
=&(T^{-1/2}XB_1 - \boldsymbol{P}([T^{-3/2}X_DB_\perp, T^{-1}X_SB_2])T^{-1/2}X_DB_1)[\eta_{1,1}, \ldots, \eta_{1,r_1}] + O_p(T^{-1/2}) \\
=&(I - \boldsymbol{P}([X_DB_\perp, X_SB_2]))T^{-1/2}XB_1[\eta_{1,1}, \ldots, \eta_{1,r_1}] + O_p(T^{-1/2}).
\end{aligned}$$

A.2.4 Proof of Proposition 3.4

We shall need the following lemma.

Lemma A.1 *Both A_T and dA are $T \times k$, possibly stochastic; for any nonstochastic, nonzero, $k \times 1$, γ, $A_T\gamma$ is $O_p(1)$ not $o_p(1)$, so that A_T has full column rank, k; dA is $O_p(T^{-\alpha}), \alpha > 0$; and ξ is arbitrary except $\| \xi \| = 1$. Then $(\boldsymbol{P}(A_T + dA) - \boldsymbol{P}(A_T))\xi$ is $O_p(T^{-\alpha})$.*

Proof. A proof is in Hatanaka (2000).

As regards Proposition 3.4,

$$\begin{aligned} \boldsymbol{P}(X) = \boldsymbol{P}([XB_\perp, XB_2, XB_1]) &= \boldsymbol{P}(XB_\perp) + \boldsymbol{P}((I - \boldsymbol{P}(XB_\perp))XB_2) \\ &\quad + \boldsymbol{P}((I - \boldsymbol{P}([XB_\perp, (I - \boldsymbol{P}(XB_\perp))XB_2]))XB_1). \end{aligned} \tag{A.18}$$

We are concerned with the three projections on the extreme RHS of (A.18). Using the above Lemma A.1 and the notation "$\approx$" defined in Section 3.5, we see that the first projection $\approx \boldsymbol{P}(X_D B_\perp)$, the second projection $\approx \boldsymbol{P}((I - \boldsymbol{P}(X_D B_\perp))X_S B_2)$, and the third projection $\approx \boldsymbol{P}(I - \boldsymbol{P}([X_D B_\perp, (I - \boldsymbol{P}\,(X_D B_\perp))X_S B_2])XB_1)$.

A.3 Mathematical Proofs of Propositions and Lemmas in Chapter 4

A.3.1 Proof of Proposition 4.2

Only one important point of the proof will be shown. In Proposition 3.2(iii) let $\gamma_{\perp,i}$, $\gamma_{2,i}$, and $\gamma_{1,i}$ be the i-th column of $\Gamma_{\perp 2}$, Γ_{22}, and Γ_{12}, respectively, so that

$$\hat{\xi}_i = B_\perp \gamma_{\perp,i} + B_2\gamma_{2,i} + B_1\gamma_{1,i}.$$

$(I - \boldsymbol{P}(\iota))X\hat{\xi}_i$ involves many terms when the above is substituted in $\hat{\xi}_i$ and $X = X_{D\perp} + X_{D*} + X_S$ is in X. Expressing $(I - \boldsymbol{P}(\iota))X$ just by X we have from (A.15)

$$\gamma_{\perp,i} = -T^{-1/2}(T^{-3}B'_\perp X'_D X_D B_\perp)^{-1}T^{-5/2}B'_\perp X'_D X_S B_2\eta_{2,i} + \delta,$$

where δ is $O_p(T^{-1})$.

$$\begin{aligned} X_D B_\perp \gamma_{\perp,i} &= -\boldsymbol{P}(X_D B_\perp)X_S B_2\eta_{2,i} + X_D B_\perp \delta \\ &= -\boldsymbol{P}(SHQ)X_S B_2\eta_{2,i} + SHQ\delta + O_p(1). \end{aligned}$$

The last equality follows from $T^{-3/2}X_D B_\perp = T^{-3/2}SHQ + O(T^{-1})$ and Lemma A.1.

A.4 Mathematical Proofs of Propositions and Lemmas in Chapter 5

A.4.1 Proof of Proposition 5.1

A.4.1.1 The Standard Time Series

It is useful to begin with the standard time series. It is easy to prove that the denominator of (5.3) converges to σ_ε^2. The major problem is why the numerator, $\Delta x'(P(Z) - P(Z_0))\Delta x$, is asymptotically σ_ε^2 times (5.7) even though it is not divided by T. x and Δx are generated by (5.8) and (5.9). Δv_{-i}, $i = 0, \ldots, k-1$, is defined in the same way as Δx_i was in the text. Since Δv_t is $AR(k)$,

$$\Delta v = a_1 \Delta v_{-1} + \cdots + a_k \Delta v_{-k} + \varepsilon, \tag{A.19}$$

where the series of ε_t is a white noise with mean zero and variance, σ_ε^2. From (5.1) and (5.2) $P(Z) - P(Z_0) = P((I - P(Z_0))Z_*)$, where $Z_* = [SH, x_{-1}]$. Z_0 includes H. Since $x_{-1} = SH\mu - H\mu + v_{-1}$, $(I - P(Z_0))x_{-1} = (I - P(Z_0))(SH\mu + v_{-1})$. Construct $\tilde{Z}_* = [SH, v_{-1}]$. The column spaces of $(I - P(Z_0))Z_*$ and $(I - P(Z_0))\tilde{Z}_*$ are identical, and $P(Z) - P(Z_0) = P((I - P(Z_0))\tilde{Z}_*)$. We reach

$$\Delta x'(P(Z) - P(Z_0))\Delta x = \Delta v' P((I - P(Z_0))\tilde{Z}_*)\Delta v.$$

Let us move to asymptotic analyses. Corresponding to the orders of different columns of $\tilde{Z}_*$, let $D_T^{-1} = \text{diag}\,[T^{-3/2} I_p, T^{-1}\sigma_v^{-1}]$, where $\sigma_v^2 = \sigma_\varepsilon^2(1 - a_1 - \cdots - a_k)^{-2}$. Noting that $\Delta x_{-i} = H\mu + \Delta v_{-i} - (H - H_{-i})\mu$ for $i = 0, 1, \ldots, k$, where $H - H_{-i}$ is $O(1)$, construct $\tilde{Z}_0 = T^{-1/2}[H, \Delta v_{-1}, \ldots, \Delta v_{-k}]$. $P(Z_0) \approx P(\tilde{Z}_0)$, where $\approx$ has been defined in Section 3.5. We obtain

$$\begin{aligned}\Delta x'(P(Z) - P(Z_0))\Delta x = \Delta v'(I - P(\tilde{Z}_0))\tilde{Z}_* D_T^{-1}(D_T^{-1}\tilde{Z}_*'(I - P(\tilde{Z}_0))\tilde{Z}_* D_T^{-1})^{-1} \\ \times D_T^{-1}\tilde{Z}_*'(I - P(\tilde{Z}_0))\Delta v + o_p(1).\end{aligned} \tag{A.20}$$

With some asymptotic analyses we see that $D_T^{-1}\tilde{Z}_*'(I - P(\tilde{Z}_0))\tilde{Z}_* D_T^{-1}$ converges to $\int_0^1 \tilde{m}(\tau)\tilde{m}(\tau)' d\tau$, where $\tilde{m}(\tau)$ is defined in (5.6) of the text. By virtue of (A.19),

$$D_T^{-1}\tilde{Z}_*'(I - P(\tilde{Z}_0))\Delta v = D_T^{-1}\tilde{Z}_*(I - P(\tilde{Z}_0))\varepsilon,$$

which converges to $\sigma_\varepsilon \int_0^1 \tilde{m}(\tau) dB(\tau)$.

A.4.1.2 The Role of Assumption 5.2

Let us turn to the principal component, (4.3) and (4.4). To begin with we shall drop $I - P(\iota)$ in (4.3). This does not affect $UURT$ in (5.3) if Assumption 5.2 is accepted. The reason is as follows. Let $x = (I - P(\iota))\hat{x}$, where $\hat{x}$ is the principal component based on the data not demeaned. Then $x_{-1} = \hat{x}_{-1}+$ a scalar multiple of ι, and $\Delta x_{-j} = \Delta\hat{x}_{-j}$, $j = 0, \ldots, k$. ($\Delta x_0 = \Delta x$.) Z and Z_0 are defined in (5.1) and (5.2). Let $\hat{Z} = [H, SH, \hat{x}_{-1}, \Delta\hat{x}_{-1}, \ldots, \Delta\hat{x}_{-k}]$, and $\hat{Z}_0 = [H, \Delta\hat{x}_{-1}, \ldots, \Delta\hat{x}_{-k}]$. Then $\boldsymbol{P}(\hat{Z}_0) = \boldsymbol{P}(Z_0)$. If ι is a column of H as assumed in Assumption 5.2, we have $\boldsymbol{P}(\hat{Z}) = \boldsymbol{P}(Z)$ in addition. With $\Delta\hat{x} = \Delta x$ we have $\Delta x'(I - \boldsymbol{P}(Z))\Delta x = \Delta\hat{x}'(I - \boldsymbol{P}(\hat{Z}))\Delta\hat{x}$, and $\Delta x'(\boldsymbol{P}(Z) - \boldsymbol{P}(Z_0))\Delta x = \Delta\hat{x}'(\boldsymbol{P}(\hat{Z}) - \boldsymbol{P}(\hat{Z}_0))\Delta\hat{x}$. It should be emphasised that the above result does not depend on any particular DGPs of x, and hence can be used in the proofs of all the propositions on $UURT$.

A.4.1.3 The Nonstandard Series

To make our notations on (4.3) and (4.4) analogous to those in (5.8) and (5.9), let us write $SHQ(\eta_{\perp,i} + \delta_{1i})$ as $SHQ\mu_1$, $X_S B_\perp \eta_{\perp,i}$ as v, and $HQ\eta_{\perp,i}$ as $H\mu_2$.

$$x = SHQ\mu_1 + v + O_p(T^{1/2}), \quad \Delta x = H\mu_2 + \Delta v + \zeta_i + O_p(T^{-1/2}). \tag{A.21}$$

Again it is easy to prove that the denominator of (5.3) converges to σ_ε^2. We shall concentrate on the numerator. Z_0 and Z_* are transformed into $\tilde{Z}_0$ and $\tilde{Z}_*$ in the same way as before. In these transformations the point that μ_1 is stochastic is not relevant. Even though (A.21) involves ζ_i defined in (4.5) in the text, $T^{-1/2}$ times lagged ζ_i can be ignored in dealing with $\boldsymbol{P}(\tilde{Z}_0)$. (A.20) now becomes

$$(\Delta v + \zeta_i)'(I - \boldsymbol{P}(\tilde{Z}_0))\tilde{Z}_* D_T^{-1}(D_T^{-1}\tilde{Z}_*'(I - \boldsymbol{P}(\tilde{Z}_0))\tilde{Z}_* D_T^{-1})^{-1} \times D_T^{-1}\tilde{Z}_*'(I - \boldsymbol{P}(\tilde{Z}_0))(\Delta v + \zeta_i) + o_p(1). \tag{A.22}$$

ζ_i is $O_p(1)$ as explained in relation to (4.5). Since (A.22) as a whole is hoped to be $O_p(1)$, we must investigate to see whether or not ζ_i can be ignored in (A.22). Fortunately we can show that $D_T^{-1}\tilde{Z}_*'(I - \boldsymbol{P}(H))\zeta_i$ converges to zero asymptotically, implying that $D_T^{-1}\tilde{Z}_*'(I - \boldsymbol{P}(\tilde{Z}_0))\zeta_i$ also converges to zero, i.e., ζ_i can be ignored in (A.22). We now prove that $D_T^{-1}\tilde{Z}_*'(I - \boldsymbol{P}(H))\zeta_i$ converges to zero. Since the RHS of (4.5) is a sum of five terms, write it as $\zeta_{1i} + \cdots + \zeta_{5i}$. It is fairly easy to prove that $D_T^{-1}\tilde{Z}_*'(I - \boldsymbol{P}(H))\zeta_{ji}, j = 1, 2, 3$ converge to zero. $D_T^{-1}\tilde{Z}_*'(I - \boldsymbol{P}(H))\zeta_{4i} = 0$. Concerning ζ_{5i}, ΔX_{D*} is derived from (2.10). In view of Definition 2.2(iv) let us explain our reasoning on the case where $h_{T,t}$ has changed only once in the sample period. $\Delta h'_{T,t} = 0$ if t is not t_0. Concerning the second term of RHS of (2.6), let $Q_j = M'B(I_r + F'B)^j(F'B)^{-1}F'$ for $j = 0, 1, \ldots$, then $\| Q_j \| = O(c^j)$, where $0 < c < 1$. Since $\Delta d'_{t*} = 0$ if $t < t_0$, and $\Delta d'_{t*} = \Delta h'_{T,t_0} Q_{t-t_0}$ if $t \geq t_0$, it follows that both $T^{-3/2}H'S'\Delta X_{D*}$ and $T^{-1}v'_{-1}\Delta X_{D*}$ converge to zero as $T \to \infty$.

A.4.2 Proof of Lemma 5.1

Only a highlight of the proof will be given. Z_* is defined in the same way as in the proof of Proposition 5.1, but $\tilde{Z}_*$ here is $[SH, u_{-1}]$. Also $\tilde{Z}_0 = [H, \Delta\boldsymbol{u}]$, where $\Delta\boldsymbol{u} = [\Delta u_{-1}, \ldots, \Delta u_{-k}]$. Let $D_T^{-1} = \text{diag}[T^{-3/2}I_p, T^{-1/2}]$. It can be shown that the numerator of $UURT$ is a quadratic form of

$$D_T^{-1}\tilde{Z}_*'(I - \boldsymbol{P}(\tilde{Z}_0))\Delta x = [0', T^{-1/2}u_{-1}'(I - \boldsymbol{P}(\Delta\boldsymbol{u}))\Delta u]' + O_p(1),$$

where $0'$ is $1 \times p$. With $\Delta\tilde{u}_t$ and $\tilde{u}_{t-1}$ defined in (5.11) and (5.12) it is seen that

$$\text{plim}_{T\to\infty} T^{-1}u_{-1}'(I - \boldsymbol{P}(\Delta\boldsymbol{u}))\Delta u = \text{cov}(\Delta\tilde{u}_t, \tilde{u}_{t-1}), \tag{A.23}$$

which is the Martingale covariance. Since the numerator of $UURT$ is asymptotically a positive definite quadratic form of $T^{-1/2}u_{-1}'(I - \boldsymbol{P}(\Delta\boldsymbol{u}))\Delta u$, it diverges to ∞ as $T \to \infty$ at the speed of T, in so far as the Martingale covariance is not zero.

A.4.3 Proof of Lemma 5.2

For the analysis of $UURT$ we may eliminate $(I - \boldsymbol{P}(\iota))$ in (4.6) by virtue of Assumption 5.2. Then (4.6) is expressed as

$$x = H\mu_0 + SHQ(\mu_1 + \delta_0) + u + V\delta_1 + O_p(1).$$

$X_S B_\perp \eta_{\perp,i}$ is I(0), and has been written u. $X_S B_\perp$ is in general I(1), and written V. μ_0 and μ_1 are nonstochastic, and δ_0 and δ_1 are $O_p(T^{-1/2})$. (4.7) is expressed as

$$\Delta x = HQ\mu_1 + \Delta u + O_p(1).$$

These are substituted in (5.3). It is easy to show that its denominator is $O_p(1)$ but not $o_p(1)$. As for the numerator, Z_* is the same as in the proof of Proposition 5.1, but $\tilde{Z}_*$ here is $[SH, u_{-1} + V_{-1}\delta_1 + O_p(1)]$. D_T^{-1} and $\tilde{Z}_0$ are the same as in the proof of Lemma 5.1. The numerator is

$$\Delta x'(I - \boldsymbol{P}(\tilde{Z}_0))\tilde{Z}_*D_T^{-1}(D_T^{-1}\tilde{Z}_*'(I - \boldsymbol{P}(\tilde{Z}_0))\tilde{Z}_*D_T^{-1})^{-1}D_T^{-1}\tilde{Z}_*'(I - \boldsymbol{P}(\tilde{Z}_0))\Delta x + O_p(1). \tag{A.24}$$

Concerning the middle portion of the quadratic form in (A.24),

$$\begin{aligned} D_T^{-1}\tilde{Z}_*'(I - \boldsymbol{P}(\tilde{Z}_0))\tilde{Z}_*D_{*T}^{-1} &= [T^{-3/2}SH, T^{-1/2}V_{-1}\delta_1]'(I - \boldsymbol{P}(H)) \\ &\times T^{-3/2}SH, T^{-1/2}V_{-1}\delta_{-1}] + \text{diag}[0, T^{-1}u_{-1}'(I - \boldsymbol{P}(\Delta\boldsymbol{u}))u_{-1}] + o_p(1). \end{aligned}$$

This is nonsingular. Concerning the right portion of the quadratic form

$$D_T^{-1}\tilde{Z}_*'(I - P(\tilde{Z}_0))\Delta x = [T^{-3/2}SH, T^{-1/2}(u_{-1} + V_{-1}\delta_2)]' \times (I - P(H) - P(\Delta u))\Delta u + O_p(1). \quad \text{(A.25)}$$

Regarding the terms involved in (A.25), both $T^{-3/2}H'S'(I - P(H) - P(\Delta u))\Delta u$ and $T^{-1/2}\delta_2'V_{-1}'(I - P(H) - P(\Delta u))\Delta u$ are $O_p(1)$, and do not diverge to ∞. In addition, $T^{-1/2}u_{-1}'P(H)\Delta u$ is $O_p(T^{-1/2})$. The only remaining term is

$$T^{-1/2}u_{-1}'(I - P(\Delta u))\Delta u. \quad \text{(A.26)}$$

Because of (A.23), (A.24) diverges if and only if the Martingale covariance is not zero.

A.4.4 Proof of Proposition 5.3

The present proof is obtained by showing that the variables in the present proposition can be transformed into some special cases of the variables in the proof of Proposition 5.1. Concerning (4.8), since

$$I - P([\iota, SHQ]) = (I - P(\iota))(I - P((I - P(\iota))SHQ)),$$

Assumption 5.2 allows us to replace $(I - P([\iota, SHQ])$ in (4.8) by $(I - P((I - P(\iota))SHQ))$ without affecting $UURT$. Henceforth $(I - P(\iota))SHQ$ will be written SHQ. Since $B_2\eta_{2,i}$ is here B_2, $n \times 1$, we write $X_S B_2 = v$. Then from (4.8) and (4.9)

$$x = (I - P(SHQ))v + \eta, \quad \Delta x = \Delta v + \zeta_i + O_p(T^{-1/2}), \quad \text{(A.27)}$$

where η is $O_p(T^{1/2})$. Consider

$$\tilde{x} = v + \eta, \quad \Delta\tilde{x} = \Delta x + H\delta, \quad \text{(A.28)}$$

where δ is $O_p(T^{-1/2})$. It is seen on the first parts of (A.27) and (A.28) that

$$x_{-1} = \tilde{x}_{-1} - SHw + Hw,$$

where $w = Q(Q'H'S'SHQ)^{-1}Q'H'S'v$. Therefore,

$$P([H, SH, \tilde{x}_{-1}, \Delta x_{-1}, \ldots, \Delta x_{-k}])$$

is identical to

$$P([H, SH, x_{-1}, \Delta x_{-1}, \ldots, \Delta x_{-k}]).$$

This identity and the second part of (A.28) can be used to prove that (A.27) and (A.28) produce the asymptotically identical $UURT$. The effects of $H\delta$ and ζ_i both vanish asymptotically. Then note that (A.28) is a special case of (A.21) such that $\mu_1 = 0$ and $\mu_2 = 0$.

A.4.5 Proof of Proposition 5.5

Write $U = X_S B_1$ and $V = X_S B_2$. From (4.10)

$$x = (I - P(\iota))(U\eta_{1,i} + H\zeta_{1i} + T^{-1/2}V\zeta_{2i} + T^{-1}SHQ\zeta_{3i} + O_p(1)), \tag{A.29}$$

where ζ_{1i}, ζ_{2i}, and ζ_{3i} are each $O_p(1)$, and $\eta_{1,i}$ is an eigenvector of U_{11}. Also from (4.11)

$$\Delta x = \Delta U\eta_{1,i} + O_p(1). \tag{A.30}$$

Assumption 5.2 allows us to drop $I - P(\iota)$ from (A.29). The denominator of $UURT$ is $O_p(1)$ not $o_p(1)$. The analysis of the numerator is analogous to the proof of Lemma 5.2.

$$\tilde{Z}_* = [SH, U_{-1}\eta_{1,i} + T^{-1/2}V_{-1}\zeta_{2i}].$$

$$\tilde{Z}_0 = T^{-1/2}[H, \Delta U_{-1}\eta_{1,i}, \ldots, \Delta U_{-k}\eta_{1,i}].$$

$$D_T^{-1} = [T^{-3/2}I_p, T^{-1/2}].$$

$$P((I - P(Z_0))Z_*) \approx P((I - P(\tilde{Z}_0))\tilde{Z}_* D_T^{-1}).$$

Regarding the quadratic form that has the same role as (A.24), the middle part,

$$D_T^{-1}\tilde{Z}_*'(I - P(\tilde{Z}_0))\tilde{Z}_* D_T^{-1},$$

is nonsingular. Among the terms in the right part, $D_T^{-1}\tilde{Z}_*'(I - P(\tilde{Z}_0))\Delta x$, all but

$$T^{-1/2}\eta_{1,i}'U_{-1}'(I - P(\Delta U_*))\Delta U\eta_{1,i} \tag{A.31}$$

are $O_p(1)$, where $\Delta U_* = [\Delta U_{-1}\eta_{1,i}, \ldots, \Delta U_{-k}\eta_{1,i}]$.

$$T^{-1}\eta_{1,i}'U_{-1}'(I - P(\Delta U_*))\Delta U\eta_{1,i} \tag{A.32}$$

is $O_p(1)$ not $o_p(1)$, and weakly converges to a random variable, which is a.s. not zero. Therefore (A.31) diverges a.s. In Lemma 5.2 $T^{-1}u_{-1}'(I - P(\Delta u))\Delta u$ had a probability limit, (A.23), and if it were zero the divergence of (A.26) would not occur. Here (A.32) is not zero a.s., and (A.31) diverges a.s.

A.4.6 Proof of Lemma 5.3

$P(Z) = P(\tilde{Z})$, $S_{00} = G'\tilde{S}_{00}G$, $S_{01} = G'\tilde{S}_{01}\operatorname{diag}[I, G]$, and

$$S_{11} = \operatorname{diag}[I, G]'\tilde{S}_{11}\operatorname{diag}[I, G].$$

Hence $\det[S_{01}S_{11}^{-1}S_{10} - \lambda S_{00}] = 0$ and $\det[\tilde{S}_{01}\tilde{S}_{11}^{-1}\tilde{S}_{10} - \lambda\tilde{S}_{00}] = 0$ share the same roots.

A.4.7 Proof of Proposition 5.6

Combining (4.8) and (4.9) over $i = 1, \ldots, r_2$, let

$$\eta_2 = [\eta_{2,1}, \ldots, \eta_{2,r_2}]$$

and

$$\zeta = [\zeta_1, \ldots, \zeta_{r_2}].$$

η_2 represents the orthonormalised eigenvectors of U_{22}. Write $V = X_S B_2$. Initially Z, (5.16), (5.17), and (5.18) are constructed by

$$X = (I - P(\iota))(I - P((I - P(\iota))SHQ))V\eta_2 + O_p(T^{1/2}) \tag{A.33}$$

$$\Delta X = \Delta V\eta_2 + \zeta + O_p(T^{-1/2}). \tag{A.34}$$

Define $\tilde{X}$ and $\Delta\tilde{X}$ by $X = (I - P(\iota))\tilde{X}$, and $\Delta X = \Delta\tilde{X}$. Assumption 5.2 allows us to replace X and ΔX by $\tilde{X}$ and $\Delta\tilde{X}$ without altering S_{00}, S_{01}, and S_{11}. Further construct $Y = \tilde{X}\eta_2^{-1}$ and $\Delta Y = \Delta\tilde{X}\eta_2^{-1}$. By virtue of Lemma 5.3, $\tilde{X}$ and $\Delta\tilde{X}$ may be replaced by Y and ΔY without altering $MURT$.

$$Y = (I - P((I - P(\iota))SHQ))V + O_p(T^{1/2}),$$
$$\Delta Y = \Delta V + \zeta\eta_2^{-1} + O_p(T^{-1/2}).$$

However S_{00}, S_{01} and S_{11} individually are affected by the transformation from $\tilde{X}$ and $\Delta\tilde{X}$ to Y and ΔY, and let S^*_{00}, S^*_{01}, and S^*_{11} be those after the transformation. We shall concentrate our explanation on

$$(T - k - 1)S^*_{01}S^{*-1}_{11}S^*_{10} = \Delta Y' P((I - P(Z))[SH, Y_{-1}])\Delta Y, \tag{A.35}$$

because it is easy to prove that $\operatorname{plim}_{T\to\infty} S^*_{00} = \Lambda$, where Λ was introduced in Assumption 5.3. $(I - P(\iota))SH$ and $(I - P(\iota))H$ will be written SH and H respectively. Since $Y_{-1} = V_{-1} - SHW + HW + O_p(T^{1/2})$, where $W = Q(Q'H'S'SHQ)^{-1}Q'H'S'V$,

$$P((I - P(Z))[SH, Y_{-1}]) = P((I - P(Z))[SH, V_{-1}]) + O_p(T^{1/2}]).$$

By virtue of Assumption 5.3, the long run covariance matrix of Δv_t is

$$\Sigma = (I - \Gamma_1 - \cdots - \Gamma_k)^{-1}\Lambda(I - \Gamma_1 - \cdots - \Gamma_k)'^{-1}. \tag{A.36}$$

For the asymptotic analyses construct $D_T^{-1} = \operatorname{diag}[T^{-3/2}I_p, T^{-1}\Sigma^{-1/2}]$, and $\tilde{Z} = T^{-1/2}[H, \Delta V_{-1}, \ldots, \Delta V_{-k}]$. Then

$$P((I - P(Z))[SH, Y_{-1}]) \approx P((I - P(\tilde{Z}))[SH, V_{-1}]D_T^{-1}).$$

Substituting this into (A.35), we see that

$$(D_T'^{-1}[SH, V_{-1}]'(I - P(\tilde{Z}))[SH, V_{-1}]D_T^{-1})^{-1}$$

weakly converges to $(\int_0^1 \tilde{M}\tilde{M}'d\tau)^{-1}$. Moreover

$$D_T'^{-1}[SH, V_{-1}]'(I - P(\tilde{Z}))(\Delta V + \zeta\eta_2^{-1} + O_p(T^{-1/2}))$$

weakly converges to $\int_0^1 \tilde{M}dB(\tau)'\Lambda'^{1/2}$. The reason why $\zeta\eta_2^{-1}$ can be ignored is the same that ζ_i can be ignored in the proof of Proposition 5.1. (See Section A.4.1.3.)

A.4.8 Proof of Proposition 5.7

We propose to prove

Statement : the weak convergence limits of the first, ..., the h-th roots of

$$\det[\lambda S_{11} - S_{10}S_{00}^{-1}S_{01}] = 0 \tag{A.37}$$

are a.s. positive, while the rest converges to zeroes.

The reason why this proves the desired result is as follows. The roots of (A.37) are the eigenvalues of

$$S_{11}^{-1/2}S_{10}S_{00}^{-1}S_{01}S_{11}^{-1/2\prime}.$$

With $A = S_{11}^{-1/2}S_{10}S_{00}^{-1/2\prime}$ and $B = S_{00}^{-1/2}S_{01}S_{11}^{-1/2\prime}$, AB and BA share the identical nonzero eigenvalues. BA is $(T - k - 1)^{-1}$ times $MURT$. If the statement holds true, the first, ..., the h-th eigenvalues of $(T - k - 1)^{-1}$ times $MURT$ are a.s. positive. The first, ..., the h-th eigenvalues of $MURT$ diverge to ∞.

The data for $MURT$ in the present proposition may be written $X = [X_2, X_{1h}]$, where X_2 is the principal components, (4.8), combined over $i = n-r+1, \ldots, n-r_1$, as expressed in (A.33). X_{1h} is (4.10) or (A.29) combined over $i = n-r_1+1, \ldots, n-r_1+h$. We write $X_{-1} = [X_{2(-1)}, X_{1h(-1)}]$. $\Delta X = [\Delta X_2, \Delta X_{1h}]$. ΔX_2 and ΔX_{1h} are in (A.34) and (A.30), respectively. $Z = [H, \Delta X_{2(-1)}, \Delta X_{1h(-1)}, \ldots, \Delta X_{2(-k)}, \Delta X_{1h(-k)}]$. Construct

$$D_T^{-1} = \begin{bmatrix} T^{-1}I_p & T^{-1}D_{p,r_2} & T^{-1}D_{p,h} \\ 0 & T^{-1/2}I_{r_2} & T^{-1/2}D_{r_2,h} \\ 0 & 0 & I_h \end{bmatrix}.$$

By choosing appropriately the above D_{p,r_2}, $D_{p,h}$, and $D_{r_2,h}$, which are each $O_p(1)$, we see that

$$T^{-1/2}(I - P(Z))[SH, X_{2(-1)}, X_{1h(-1)}]D_T^{-1}$$
$$\approx (I - P(Z))[T^{-3/2}SH, T^{-1}V_{-1}\eta_2, T^{-1/2}U_{-1}\eta_{1(h)}],$$

where $V = X_S B_2$, $U = X_S B_1$, and $\eta_{1(h)} = [\eta_{1,1}, \ldots, \eta_{1,h}]$. The above is substituted in S_{01} and S_{11} as specified in (5.17) and (5.18) in the text. The roots of (A.37) are the roots of

$$\det[\lambda D_T^{-1\prime} S_{11} D_T^{-1} - D_T^{-1\prime} S_{10} S_{00}^{-1} S_{01} D_T^{-1}] = 0. \tag{A.38}$$

We can show that $D_T^{-1\prime} S_{11} D_T^{-1}$ weakly converges to the form,

$$\begin{bmatrix} A_{p,p} & A_{p,r_2} & 0 \\ A_{r_2,p} & A_{r_2,r_2} & 0 \\ 0 & 0 & A_{h,h} \end{bmatrix}, \tag{A.39}$$

and that $D_T^{-1\prime} S_{10} S_{00}^{-1} S_{01} D_T^{-1}$ weakly converges to the form,

$$\begin{bmatrix} 0 & 0 & 0 \\ 0 & 0 & 0 \\ 0 & 0 & B_h' C^{-1} B_h \end{bmatrix}. \tag{A.40}$$

The submatrices that are zero in (A.39) are due to

$$[T^{-3/2}SH, T^{-1}V_{-1}\eta_2]'(I - P(Z))[T^{-1/2}U_{-1}\eta_{1(h)}] \to 0.$$

In (A.40) the submatrices other than $B_h' C^{-1} B_h$ are zero because $S_{01} D_T^{-1}$ weakly converges to the form, $[0, 0, B_h]$, and the zeroes in $[0, 0, B_h]$ are due to

$$T^{-1/2}[\Delta V\eta_2 + \zeta, \Delta U\eta_{1(h)}]'(I - P(Z))[T^{-3/2}SH, T^{-1}V_{-1}\eta_2] \to 0.$$

By virtue of (A.39) and (A.40), the content of $[\cdot]$ in (A.38) asymptotically consists of two diagonally located blocks; the first block, which is $(p + r_2) \times (p + r_2)$, is

$$\lambda \begin{bmatrix} A_{p,p} & A_{p,r_2} \\ A_{r_2,p} & A_{r_2,r_2} \end{bmatrix} \equiv \lambda A,$$

and the second block, which is $h \times h$, is $\lambda A_{h,h} - B_h' C^{-1} B_h$. (A.38) is asymptotically

$$\det[\lambda A] \det[\lambda A_{h,h} - B_h' C^{-1} B_h] = 0.$$

A is nonsingular, because it is the weak convergence limit of

$$[T^{-3/2}SH, T^{-1}V_{-1}\eta_2]'(I - P(H))[T^{-3/2}SH, T^{-1}V_{-1}\eta_2].$$

Asymptotically (A.38) has zero roots in multiplicity, $p + r_2$. The remaining h roots of (A.38) are asymptotically the roots of

$$\det[\lambda A_{h,h} - B_h' C^{-1} B_h] = 0. \tag{A.41}$$

Let $\tilde{Z} = [\Delta V_{-1}\eta_2, \Delta U_{-1}\eta_{1(h)}, \ldots, \Delta V_{-k}\eta_2, \Delta U_{-k}\eta_{1(h)}]$. $A_{h,h}$ is the weak convergence limit of $T^{-1}\eta_{1(h)}' U_{-1}'(I - P(\tilde{Z}))U_{-1}\eta_{1(h)}$, and the limit is a.s. nonsingular. For a $h \times 1$ vector, γ, $B_h\gamma$ is the weak convergence limit of $T^{-1}[\Delta V\eta_2, \Delta U\eta_{1(h)}]'(I - P(\tilde{Z}))U_{-1}\eta_{1(h)}\gamma$, which is a.s. not zero for any γ. C is the weak convergence limit of

$$S_{00} \approx T^{-1}[\Delta V\eta_2, \Delta U\eta_{1(h)}]'(I - P(\tilde{Z}))[\Delta V\eta_2, \Delta\eta_{1(h)}],$$

and it is positive definite. Thus we have reached the conclusion that both $A_{h,h}$ and $B_h' C^{-1} B_h$ are positive definite. The roots of (A.41) are a.s. positive. (Indeed they are less than 1 because $A_{h,h} - B_h' C^{-1} B_h$ is positive definite.) We have proved the Statement which was introduced at the beginning of the present proof.

A.4.9 Proof of Lemma 5.4

Let

$$U_{t-1} = [u_{t-1}, \Delta u_{t-1}, \ldots, \Delta u_{t-k}]', \quad (k + 1) \times 1.$$

In the linear process the conditional expectation is represented by the projection. Projecting Δu_t on U_{t-1},

$$\alpha = (\mathrm{E}(U_{t-1}U_{t-1}'))^{-1}\,\mathrm{E}(U_{t-1}\Delta u_t), \quad (k + 1) \times 1 \tag{A.42}$$

$$\mathrm{E}(\Delta u_t \mid U_{t-1}) = \alpha' U_{t-1}.$$

$\mathrm{E}(U_{t-1}U_{t-1}')$ is nonsingular for any k because the series of u_t is indeterministic. Construct

$$\eta_t = \Delta u_t - \mathrm{E}(\Delta u_t \mid U_{t-1}). \tag{A.43}$$

Then

$$\Delta u_t = \alpha' U_{t-1} + \eta_t. \tag{A.44}$$

$\tilde{u}_{t-1}$ is defined in (5.12) in the text. Noting that $\tilde{u}_{t-1}$ and $[\Delta u_{t-1}, \ldots, \Delta u_{t-k}]$ are both linearly related to elements of U_{t-1}, and considering (A.43), we have both

$$\mathrm{E}(\tilde{u}_{t-1}\eta_t) = 0, \tag{A.45}$$

and

$$\mathrm{E}([\Delta u_{t-1}, \ldots, \Delta u_{t-k}]\eta_t) = 0. \tag{A.46}$$

Write $\alpha' = [\alpha_0, \alpha_1, \ldots, \alpha_k]$. Taking expectations of both sides of (A.44) conditional upon $[\Delta u_{t-1}, \ldots, \Delta u_{t-k}]$, and using (A.46), which implies $\mathrm{E}(\eta_t \mid \Delta u_{t-1}, \ldots, \Delta u_{t-k}) = 0$,

$$\mathrm{E}(\Delta u_t \mid \Delta u_{t-1}, \ldots, \Delta u_{t-k}) = \alpha_0 \, \mathrm{E}(u_{t-1} \mid \Delta u_{t-1}, \ldots, \Delta u_{t-k}) + \alpha_1 \Delta u_{t-1} + \cdots + \alpha_k \Delta u_{t-k}. \quad \text{(A.47)}$$

Subtracting (A.47) from (A.44),

$$\Delta \tilde{u}_t = \alpha_0 \tilde{u}_{t-1} + \eta_t, \quad \text{(A.48)}$$

where $\Delta \tilde{u}_t$ is defined in (5.11). By virtue of (A.45), the multiplication of both sides of (A.48) by $\tilde{u}_{t-1}$ leads to $\mathrm{cov}(\Delta \tilde{u}_t, \tilde{u}_{t-1}) = \alpha_0 \, \mathrm{var}(\tilde{u}_{t-1})$. Thus $\mathrm{cov}(\Delta \tilde{u}_t, \tilde{u}_{t-1}) = 0$ if and only if $\alpha_0 = 0$. Let D be $(k+1) \times (k+1)$, having $1, -1, \ldots, -1$ on the diagonal line, $1, \ldots, 1$ one line below, and zero elsewhere. Also let $U^*_{t-1} = [u_{t-1}, \ldots, u_{t-k-1}]$. Then $U_{t-1} = DU^*_{t-1}$. From (A.42) α_0 is the first element of

$$(D \, \mathrm{E}(U^*_{t-1}(U^*_{t-1})')D')^{-1} D \, \mathrm{E}(U^*_{t-1}(u_t - u_{t-1})).$$

The first row of D'^{-1} is ι'_{k+1}. The first element of

$$(D \, \mathrm{E}(U^*_{t-1}(U^*_{t-1})')D')^{-1} D \, \mathrm{E}(U^*_{t-1} u_t)$$

is τ_{k+1} in (5.20) in the text. The first element of

$$(D \, \mathrm{E}(U^*_{t-1}(U^*_{t-1})')D')^{-1} D \, \mathrm{E}(U^*_{t-1} u_{t-1})$$

is 1. $\alpha_0 = 0$ if and only if $\tau_{k+1} = 1$.

A.5 Mathematical Proofs of Propositions and Lemmas in Chapter 6

A.5.1 Proof of Lemma 6.1

$$(I - \boldsymbol{P}(SHQ))\boldsymbol{P}([H, SH])(I - \boldsymbol{P}(SHQ)) = \boldsymbol{P}([H, SH]) - \boldsymbol{P}(SHQ)\boldsymbol{P}([H, SH]) - \boldsymbol{P}([H, SH])\boldsymbol{P}(SHQ) + \boldsymbol{P}(SHQ)\boldsymbol{P}([H, SH])\boldsymbol{P}(SHQ).$$

On the RHS the second and the third terms are each $-\boldsymbol{P}(SHQ)$, and the fourth term is $\boldsymbol{P}(SHQ)$, because $\boldsymbol{P}([H, SH]) = \boldsymbol{P}(SH) + \boldsymbol{P}((I - \boldsymbol{P}(SH))H)$, and $\boldsymbol{P}(SHQ) = \boldsymbol{P}(SHQ)\boldsymbol{P}(SH) = \boldsymbol{P}(SH)\boldsymbol{P}(SHQ)$.

A.5.2 Proof of Proposition 6.2

Here H and SH are demeaned as pointed out in the text. Z is the r_2 principal components in Group 2, which are (4.8) combined over $i = n - r + 1, \ldots, n - r_1$. Since $I - \boldsymbol{P}([\iota, SHQ])$ in (4.8) is $(I - \boldsymbol{P}((I - \boldsymbol{P}(\iota))SHQ))(I - \boldsymbol{P}(\iota))$, it is $(I - \boldsymbol{P}(SHQ))(I - \boldsymbol{P}(\iota))$ in the present notation of SH. Write $V = X_S B_2$, which is I(1), not cointegrated. Then

$$Z = (I - \boldsymbol{P}(SHQ))(I - \boldsymbol{P}(\iota))V\eta_2 + O_p(T^{1/2}).$$

V has a nonsingular long run covariance matrix, Σ in (A.36). It is Cholesky decomposed as $\Sigma^{1/2}\Sigma^{1/2\prime}$. Since the eigenvalues of TRT are invariant through linear transformations of Z, we may postmultiply Z by $\eta_2^{-1}\Sigma^{-1/2\prime}$.

$$Z = (I - \boldsymbol{P}(SHQ))(I - \boldsymbol{P}(\iota))V\Sigma^{-1/2\prime} + O_p(T^{1/2}). \tag{A.49}$$

Construct $A = T^{-2}Z'\boldsymbol{P}([H, SH])Z$ and $B = T^{-2}Z'(I - \boldsymbol{P}([H, SH]))Z$. Then TRT in (6.2) is $B^{-1/2}AB'^{-1/2}$. Substituting (A.49) into A,

$$\begin{aligned} A = T^{-2}\Sigma^{-1/2}V'(I - \boldsymbol{P}(\iota))(I - \boldsymbol{P}(SHQ))\boldsymbol{P}([H, SH]) \\ \times (I - \boldsymbol{P}(SHQ))(I - \boldsymbol{P}(\iota))V\Sigma^{-1/2\prime} + o_p(1). \end{aligned}$$

It follows from Lemma 6.1 that

$$A = T^{-2}\Sigma^{-1/2}V'(I - \boldsymbol{P}(\iota))(\boldsymbol{P}([H, SH]) - \boldsymbol{P}(SHQ))(I - \boldsymbol{P}(\iota))V\Sigma^{-1/2\prime} + o_p(1),$$

and, this weakly converges to $(V_1 - V_2)$, where V_1 and V_2 are defined in (6.5) and (6.6). Likewise

$$\begin{aligned} B &= T^{-2}\Sigma^{-1/2}V'(I - \boldsymbol{P}(\iota))(I - \boldsymbol{P}(SHQ))(I - \boldsymbol{P}([H, SH])(I - \boldsymbol{P}(SHQ)) \\ &\quad \times (I - \boldsymbol{P}(\iota))V\Sigma^{-1/2\prime} + o_p(1) \\ &= T^{-2}\Sigma^{-1/2}V'(I - \boldsymbol{P}(\iota))(I - \boldsymbol{P}([H, SH])(I - \boldsymbol{P}(\iota))V\Sigma^{-1/2\prime} + o_p(1), \end{aligned}$$

where the second equality has been derived from Lemma 6.1. B weakly converges to $(V_0 - V_1)$. The conclusion is that TRT weakly converges to (6.3). QED

The following lemma provides preparation for the proofs of propositions on the reduced rank regression of X on SH. Q_* is defined in (6.17) in the text. $[Q, Q_\perp]$ is a $p \times p$ orthogonal matrix.

Lemma A.2

$$Q_\perp'(H'S'SH)^{-1}Q_\perp = (Q_*'H'S'SHQ_*)^{-1}, \tag{A.50}$$

$$Q_\perp'(H'S'SH)^{-1} = (Q_*'H'S'SHQ_*)^{-1}Q_*'. \tag{A.51}$$

Proof. (A.50) is proved as follows.

$$
\begin{aligned}
&Q'_\perp(H'S'SH)^{-1}Q_\perp Q'_* H'S'SHQ_*\\
=&Q'_\perp(H'S'SH)^{-1}Q_\perp Q'_\perp H'S'(I-\boldsymbol{P}(SHQ))SHQ_\perp\\
=&Q'_\perp(H'S'SH)^{-1}(I-QQ')H'S'(I-\boldsymbol{P}(SHQ))SHQ_\perp\\
=&Q'_\perp(H'S'SH)^{-1}H'S'(I-\boldsymbol{P}(SHQ))SHQ_\perp,
\end{aligned}
$$

which is equal to $Q'_\perp Q_\perp = I$ because $Q'_\perp(H'S'SH)^{-1}H'S'\boldsymbol{P}(SHQ) = 0$. (A.51) is proved as follows.

$$
\begin{aligned}
&(Q'_* H'S'SHQ_*)^{-1}Q'_* = Q'_\perp(H'S'SH)^{-1}Q_\perp Q'_*\\
=&Q'_\perp(H'S'SH)^{-1}(I-H'S'SHQ(Q'H'S'SHQ)^{-1}Q')\\
=&Q'_\perp(H'S'SH)^{-1},
\end{aligned}
$$

where the second equality is derived from

$$
\begin{aligned}
Q_\perp Q'_* &= Q_\perp Q'_\perp - Q_\perp Q'_\perp H'S'SHQ(Q'H'S'SHQ)^{-1}Q'\\
&= Q_\perp Q'_\perp - (I-QQ')H'S'SHQ(Q'H'S'SHQ)^{-1}Q'\\
&= Q'_\perp Q'_\perp - H'S'SHQ(Q'H'S'SHQ)^{-1}Q' + QQ'\\
&= I - H'S'SHQ(Q'H'S'SHQ)^{-1}Q'.
\end{aligned}
$$

A.5.3 Proof of Lemma 6.2

We are concerned with the eigenvalues and eigenvectors of (6.16). $Y = [Y_\perp, Y_2, Y_1]$ is defined in (6.10), (6.11), and (6.12). $U = [U_2, U_1]$ is defined in the text through $[Y_2, Y_1]$. Because of (6.19) $\boldsymbol{P}(Y) = \boldsymbol{P}(SHQ) + \boldsymbol{P}(U)$, and $\boldsymbol{P}(U) = UU'$. Thus (6.16) is $F_\perp + F_*$, where

$$
\begin{aligned}
F_\perp &= (H'S'SH)^{-1/2}H'S'\boldsymbol{P}(SHQ)SH(H'S'SH)'^{-1/2}\\
&= (H'S'SH)'^{1/2}Q(Q'H'S'SHQ)^{-1}Q'(H'S'SH)^{1/2},
\end{aligned}
$$

and

$$
F_* = (H'S'SH)^{-1/2}H'S'UU'SH(H'S'SH)'^{-1/2}.
$$

A.5.3.1 Proof of Lemma 6.2(i)

$F_\perp$ is idempotent with rank $n-r$. The eigenvalues are 1 with multiplicity, $n-r$, and zero with multiplicity, $p-n+r$. Concerning $\tilde{\xi}_\perp$ in (6.20) we can verify that $F_\perp\tilde{\xi}_\perp = \tilde{\xi}_\perp$, i.e., columns of $\tilde{\xi}_\perp$ are eigenvectors of $F_\perp$ which correspond to the eigenvalue, 1. (6.19) leads to $F_*\tilde{\xi}_\perp = 0$. Thus $(F_\perp + F_*)\tilde{\xi}_\perp = \tilde{\xi}_\perp$. Columns of $\tilde{\xi}_\perp$ are eigenvectors of (not only $F_\perp$ but also) $F_\perp + F_*$, and the corresponding eigenvalues of $F_\perp + F_*$ are 1 with multiplicity, $n-r$.

A.5.3.2 Proof of Lemma 6.2(ii)

Nonzero eigenvalues of F_* are nonzero eigenvalues of $U'\boldsymbol{P}(SH)U$. By virtue of (6.19) and (6.18), $U'\boldsymbol{P}(SH)U = U'\boldsymbol{P}(SHQ_*)U$. Therefore, positive eigenvalues of F_* are positive eigenvalues of $U'\boldsymbol{P}(SHQ_*)U$, i.e., diagonal elements of Λ_*. Concerning $\tilde{\xi}_*$ in (6.21) we can use (A.50) and (A.51) to show $\tilde{\xi}_*'\tilde{\xi}_* = I$ and $\tilde{\xi}_*'F_*\tilde{\xi}_* = \Lambda_*$, respectively. Thus $\tilde{\xi}_*$ represents ortho-normalised eigenvectors of F_* that correspond to its positive eigenvalues lying on the diagonal of Λ_*. It is easy to see that $F_\perp\tilde{\xi}_* = 0$ so that $\tilde{\xi}_*$ is the ortho-normalised eigenvectors of $F_\perp + F_*$ that correspond to the positive eigenvalues, Λ_*.

A.5.3.3 Proof of Lemma 6.2(iii)

We shall show that the eigenvalues of $F_\perp + F_*$ derived in A.5.3.2 above are a.s. smaller than the eigenvalues in A.5.3.1 above, which are 1. Since $U'\boldsymbol{P}(SHQ_*)U \leq U'U \equiv I_r$, the eigenvalues of $U'\boldsymbol{P}(SHQ_*)U$ cannot exceed 1. If an eigenvalue of $U'\boldsymbol{P}(SHQ_*)U$ is 1, there must exist η such that $\eta'\eta = 1$ and $\eta'U'\boldsymbol{P}(SHQ_*)U\eta = 1$, i.e., $\eta'U'U\eta = \eta'U'\boldsymbol{P}(SHQ_*)U\eta$ in probability 1, implying that $U\eta$ is a.s. contained in $\text{csp}(SHQ_*)$. This cannot hold true. The conclusion is that the eigenvalues of $U'\boldsymbol{P}(SHQ_*)U$ are less than 1 in probability 1.

A.5.4 Proof of Lemma 6.3

A.5.4.1 Proof of Lemma 6.3(iii)

Because of (6.8) and (6.21) the part of $\hat{Q}_{(q)}$ other than $\hat{Q}_{(n-r)}$ is

$$(T^{-3}H'S'SH)^{-1}Q_\perp T^{-3/2}Q_*'H'S'U\Omega_*\Lambda_*^{-1/2}[I_{q-n+r}, 0]]'.$$

The part of (6.24) other than $\hat{Q}_{(n-r)}$ is obtained by (A.51) in Lemma A.2.

A.5.5 Proof of Proposition 6.4

A.5.5.1 Proof of Proposition 6.4(iii)

Let $\hat{Q}_{*,q-n+r} = (T^{-3}H'S'SH)'^{-1/2}[\hat{\xi}_{n-r+1}, \ldots, \hat{\xi}_q]$ so that $\hat{Q}_{(q)} = [\hat{Q}_{(n-r)}, \hat{Q}_{*,q-n+r}]$ in (6.8). $\hat{Q}_{*,q-n+r}$ weakly converges to Q_*W_* by virtue of (6.24), where $W_* = N_{**}^{-1}V_*\Omega_*\Lambda_*^{-1/2}[I_{q-n+r}, 0']'$. $\text{csp}(\hat{Q}_{(q)})$ converges to $\text{csp}(Q, Q_*W_{*,q-n+r})$, but

$$\begin{aligned}\text{csp}(Q, Q_*W_{*,q-n+r}) &= \text{csp}(Q) + \text{csp}((I - \boldsymbol{P}(Q))Q_*W_{*,q-n+r}) \\ &= \text{csp}(Q) + \text{csp}(Q_\perp W_{*,q-n+r}).\end{aligned}$$

A.5.6 Proof of Lemma 6.4

As shown in (6.8) the first q_1 columns of $\hat{Q}_{(q_2)}$ are identical to $\hat{Q}_{(q_1)}$, and $\hat{Q}_{(q_2)}$ has additional columns that are linearly independent of those of $\hat{Q}_{(q_1)}$. Therefore, in probability 1 in the probability measure of $\tilde{B}$, $M(\hat{Q}_{(q_1)}, d(\tilde{B})) - M(\hat{Q}_{(q_2)}, d(\tilde{B}))$ is positive definite, and $\lambda_1(M(\hat{Q}_{(q_1)}, d(\tilde{B}))) > \lambda_1(M(\hat{Q}_{(q_2)}, d(\tilde{B})))$. Thus, dropping $d(\tilde{B})$ from the notation of M,

$$\Pr[\lambda_1(M(\hat{Q}_{(q_1)})) \geq \hat{C}_{(q_2)}(\alpha, d(\tilde{B}))] > \Pr[\lambda_1(M(\hat{Q}_{(q_2)})) \geq \hat{C}_{(q_2)}(\alpha, d(\tilde{B}))] \equiv \alpha.$$

To have $\Pr[\lambda_1(M(\hat{Q}_{(q_1)})) \geq \hat{C}_{(q_1)}(\alpha, d(\tilde{B}))] = \alpha$, we must have $\hat{C}_{(q_1)}(\alpha, d(\tilde{B})) > \hat{C}_{(q_2)}(\alpha, d(\tilde{B}))$.

A.5.7 Proof of Proposition 6.5

(a) By virtue of Proposition 6.4(i), $M(Q, r_2) - M(\hat{Q}_{(n-r)}, r_2)$ is $O_p(T^{-1/2})$ in the probability measure of X_S, and so is $\lambda_1(M(Q, r_2)) - \lambda_1(M(\hat{Q}_{(n-r)}, r_2))$. (b) The probability distributions of $\lambda_1(M(Q, r_2))$ and $\lambda_1(M(\hat{Q}_{(n-r)}, r_2))$ are generated by the probability measure of $\tilde{B}$ with Q and $\hat{Q}_{(n-r)}$ fixed. These distributions have continuous density functions because $\tilde{B}$ is Gaussian. (c) Compare the upper α points in these distributions of $\lambda_1(M(\hat{Q}_{(n-r)}, r_2))$ and $\lambda_1(M(Q, r_2))$. The above (a) and (b) suggest that $\hat{C}_{(n-r)}(\alpha, r_2) - C_Q(\alpha, r_2)$ is $O_p(T^{-1/2})$ in the probability measure of X_S, proving (i) of the proposition. (d) Proposition 6.2 and (i) of the present proposition proves (ii).

A.5.8 Proof of Proposition 6.7

A.5.8.1 Proof of Proposition 6.7(i)

Consider $M(r_a) \equiv (V_0 - V_1)^{-1/2} V_1 (V_0 - V_1)'^{-1/2}$, where V_0 and V_1 are those in (6.4) and (6.5) with r_a-dimensional $\tilde{B}$. Notice that V_2 and hence Q are not involved in $M(r_a)$. On the other hand $M(\hat{Q}_{(n-r-h)}, r_a)$ is (6.3) in which Q is fixed at $\hat{Q}_{(n-r-h)}$ in (6.6). $M(r_a) - M(\hat{Q}_{(n-r-h)}, r_a)$ is positive semi-definite in probability 1 in the probability measure of $\tilde{B}$. $\lambda_1(M(r_a)) \geq \lambda_1(M(\hat{Q}_{(n-r-h)}, r_a))$ in probability 1.

$$\Pr[\lambda_1(M(r_a)) \geq \hat{C}_{(n-r-h)}(\alpha, r_a)] \geq \alpha,$$

and $\hat{C}_{(n-r-h)}(\alpha, r_a)$ cannot exceed the upper α point in the distribution of $\lambda_1(M(r_a))$. The latter is bounded, and so is the former.

A.5.8.2 Proof of Proposition 6.7(ii)

$Z = (I - P(\iota))X[\hat{\xi}_{n-r-h+1}, \ldots, \hat{\xi}_{n-r-h+r_a}]$ is substituted in (6.2). If $n-r-h+r_a > n-r$, Z is

$$(I - P(\iota))[SHQB_{\perp}\eta_{\perp,n-r-h+1}, \ldots, SHQB_{\perp}\eta_{\perp,n-r}, 0, \ldots, 0] + O_p(T)$$

by virtue of (4.3), (4.6), (4.8), and (4.10). If $n - r - h + r_a \leq n - r$, Z is

$$(I - \boldsymbol{P}(\iota))[SHQB_{\perp}\eta_{\perp,n-r-h+1}, \ldots, SHQB_{\perp}\eta_{\perp,n-r-h+r_a}] + O_p(T).$$

In both cases the maximum eigenvalue of TRT diverges to ∞ as $T \to \infty$.

B OLS Inference on the Matrix B

The co-trending rank, r, has been determined from the time series data. Unless the result is $r = 0$, researchers are concerned with the inference on the $n \times r$ coefficients matrix, B, with the r that has been obtained. In the present appendix we set forth

Assumption B.1 *r, r_2, and r_1 are a priori known, and $r > 0$.*

Assumption B.2 *Assumptions 2.1 and 2.2 in Chapter 2 hold.*

Assumption B.1 means that the following analyses will ignore the error that may possibly have been incurred in the results of the sequential decision. All the results on deterministic trends in Chapter 2 and the notations in (2.9), (2.7), and (4.1) will be used. In particular

$$X = X_D + X_S, \quad X_D = SHQB'_{\perp} + HK + O(1), \tag{B.1}$$

where $SHQB'_{\perp}B = 0$, $SHQB'_{\perp}B_{\perp} = SHQ$ is $O(T^{3/2})$, and HK is $O(T^{1/2})$. Even though B represents relations among deterministic trends, the inference on B requires analyses of the stochastic part, X_S. We introduce

Assumption B.3 *The series of s_t is generated by a possibly cointegrated I(1) process, which has been developed by the Granger representation theorem in Engle and Granger (1987).*

Johansen (1988) constructed an important inference method for the model of cointegrated I(1) process. Most of the notations therein will be adopted except for our r_* and C^* shown below. In the VMA representation

$$s_t = C(1)\sum_{s=1}^{t} \varepsilon_s + C^*(L)\varepsilon_t, \tag{B.2}$$

which is derived from $\Delta s_t = C(L)\varepsilon_t$. Here the sequence of ε_t is an n-dimensional i.i.d. process with $E(\varepsilon_t\varepsilon_t') = \Lambda$, and $C(L) = C_0 + C_1L + C_2L^2 + \cdots$, $C^*(L) = (C(L) - C(1))/(1 - L) = C_0^* + C_1^*L + C_2^*L^2 + \cdots$. In the Error Correction VAR representation

$$\Delta s_t = \alpha\beta' s_{t-1} + \Gamma_1 \Delta s_{t-1} + \cdots + \Gamma_k \Delta s_{t-k} + \varepsilon_t, \tag{B.3}$$

where $\text{rank}(\alpha) = \text{rank}(\beta) = r_*$ and $\text{rank}(C(1)) = n - r_*$. Important connections between the two representations due to the Granger representation theorem are

$$C(1)'\beta = 0, \quad C(1)\alpha = 0. \tag{B.4}$$

Assumption B.4 *The $r \times r$ submatrix of B that consists of the first r rows is nonsingular.*

This assumption allows a normalisation of B,

$$N(B) \equiv \begin{bmatrix} I_r \\ -B_{n-r} \end{bmatrix}.$$

B_{n-r} is $(n-r) \times r$, and we shall be concerned with the inference on B_{n-r} on the basis of OLS.(14) The cases where $r_2 > 0$ and $r_2 = 0$ are examined separately. The results in the present appendix will be presented without proofs. The Brownian motion process will be indicated by $W(\cdot)$ instead of $B(\cdot)$.

B.1 The Case Where $r_2 > 0$

Each of X, X_D, and X_S is partitioned into its first r columns and the remaining $n - r$ columns, so that $X = [X_r, X_{n-r}]$, $X_D = [X_{D,r}, X_{D,n-r}]$, and $X_S = [X_{S,r}, X_{S,n-r}]$. Note that $X_D N(B) = X_{D,r} - X_{D,n-r} B_{n-r}$ is only $O(T^{1/2})$ by virtue of Assumption 2.1(a). Moreover, for any non-zero γ, $X_{D,n-r}\gamma$ is $O(T^{3/2})$ not $o(T^{3/2})$. This is due to Assumption 2.1(b) and the fact that Assumption B.4 does not allow $[0', \gamma']'$ to belong to csp(B). $\lim_{T\to\infty} T^{-3} X'_{D,n-r} X_{D,n-r}$ is nonsingular. These points suggest the following OLS,

$$\hat{B}_{n-r} = (X'_{n-r} X_{n-r})^{-1} X'_{n-r} X_r.$$

To develop an asymptotic analysis of $\hat{B}_{n-r}$, let $g(\tau)$ be the continuous time representation of SH as defined in Section 5.1. Since $T^{-3/2} X_{D,n-r} = T^{-3/2} SHQB'_{\perp}[0, I_{n-r}]'$ $+ O(T^{-1})$ in the notations in (B.1), the continuous time representation of $T^{-3/2} X_{D,n-r}$ is

$$D_{n-r}(\tau) = [0, I_{n-r}] B_{\perp} Q' g(\tau), \quad 1 \geq \tau \geq 0.$$

Let G_B, $r \times r_1$, be as defined in Section 3.1 (while replacing B there by $N(B)$), and let G_* be $r \times r_2$ such that $G = [G_B, G_*]$ is $r \times r$ nonsingular. As indicated in Lemma 3.1, $N(B)G_B$ is in csp(β) but $N(B)G_*$ is not. $X_S N(B) G_*$ is I(1), not cointegrated.

Proposition B.1 *When* $r_2 > 0$,

$$T^{1/2}(\hat{B}_{n-r} - B_{n-r})G \xrightarrow{w} [0, VG_*], \tag{B.5}$$

where 0 *has* r_1 *columns,*

$$V = (\int_0^1 D_{n-r}D'_{n-r}d\tau)^{-1} \int_0^1 D_{n-r}W'd\tau\Lambda^{1/2}C(1)'N(B), \tag{B.6}$$

and $W(\tau)$ *is the n-dimensional, standard Brownian motion process.*

In fact $T^{1/2}(\hat{B}_{n-r} - B_{n-r})$ converges to V. V does not have full column rank, r, but only $r - r_1$, when $r_1 > 0$. This is because $C(1)'N(B)G_B = 0$ by virtue of (B.4) and the fact that $N(B)G_B$ is in csp(β). Proposition B.1 has made this fact apparent. When $r_1 = 0$, the matrix 0 vanishes from the RHS of (B.5).

Lemma B.1 vec(VG_*) *in* (B.5) *is asymptotically distributed in the normal distribution with mean zero and the covariance matrix,* $\Sigma_1 \otimes \Sigma_2$, *where*

$$\Sigma_1 = G'_*N(B)'C(1)\Lambda C(1)'N(B)G_*,$$

$$\Sigma_2 = (\int_0^1 D_{n-r}D'_{n-r}d\tau)^{-1} \int_0^1 \int_0^1 \min(\tau_1, \tau_2)D_{n-r}(\tau_1)D_{n-r}(\tau_2)'d\tau_1 d\tau_2 \times (\int_0^1 D_{n-r}D'_{n-r}d\tau)^{-1}.$$

Let us turn to the hypothesis testing. Any linear hypothesis can be expressed as

$$A\,\mathrm{vec}(B_{n-r}) = a, \tag{B.7}$$

where A is a $q \times r(n-r)$ known matrix with its full row rank, and a, $q \times 1$, is also known. Since $T^{1/2}(\hat{B}_{n-r} - B_{n-r})G_B$ converges to zero as indicated in (B.5), our asymptotic testing in effect tests a hypothesis on $B_{n-r}G_*$, treating $\hat{B}_{n-r}G_B$ as though it were the true value of $B_{n-r}G_B$. This can be seen as follows. For simplicity let us assume that $G'_BG_B = I_{r_1}$, $G'_*G_* = I_{r_2}$, and $G'_*G_B = 0$ so that G is an orthogonal matrix. If (B.7) holds true, $T^{1/2}(A\,\mathrm{vec}(\hat{B}_{n-r}) - a)$ is asymptotically equivalent to $A\,\mathrm{vec}(T^{1/2}(\hat{B}_{n-r} - B_{n-r})G_*G'_*)$, which is what we would have if we test the hypothesis, $A\,\mathrm{vec}(B_{n-r}G_*G'_*) = b$, where $b = a - A\,\mathrm{vec}(B_{n-r}G_BG'_B)$. Concerning the test of (B.7) with $\hat{B}_{n-r}$,

Proposition B.2 *If* $r_2 > 0$ *and the hypothesis* (B.7) *holds true,* $T^{1/2}(A\,\mathrm{vec}(\hat{B}_{n-r}) - a)$ *is asymptotically distributed in the normal distribution with mean zero and the covariance matrix,*

$$\Sigma_3 = A(G_*\Sigma_1G'_* \otimes \Sigma_2)A'. \tag{B.8}$$

Note that $G_* \Sigma_1 G'_*$, involving $G_* G'_*$, has rank default in so far as $r_1 > 0$. If the hypothesis (B.7) holds true, and if Σ_3 can be consistently estimated by $\hat{\Sigma}_3$ under the hypothesis,

$$T(A\,\mathrm{vec}(\hat{B}_{n-r}) - a)'\hat{\Sigma}_3^{-1}(A\,\mathrm{vec}(\hat{B}_{n-r}) - a)$$

should be distributed asymptotically in the χ^2 distribution with q degrees of freedom. As for the consistent estimation of Σ_3, B_{n-r} is estimated by $\hat{B}_{n-r}$, and $B'_\perp Q$ in $D_{n-r}(\tau)$ is estimated by $\hat{R}'_{(n-r)}\hat{Q}_{(n-r)}$ given in (6.8) and (6.9). Estimation of G_*, $C(1)$, and Λ will be discussed later in the present appendix.(15)

B.2 The Case Where $r_2 = 0$

When $r_2 = 0$, $T^{1/2}(\hat{B}_{n-r} - B_{n-r})$ converges to zero because $C(1)'N(B) = 0$ in (B.6). To emphasise that $r = r_1$ here X_r, X_{n-r}, $X_{D,r}$, $X_{D,n-r}$, B_{n-r}, and $N(B)$ will be written respectively as X_{r_1}, X_{n-r_1}, X_{D,r_1}, $X_{D,n-r_1}$, B_{n-r_1}, and $N(B_1)$. Note that since $X_{D\perp}N(B_1) = 0$,

$$X_D N(B_1) = X_{D,r_1} - X_{D,n-r_1}B_{n-r_1} = X_{D*}N(B_1) = HKN(B_1) + O(1)$$

in the notations of (B.1). Thus

$$(I - \boldsymbol{P}(H))(X_{D,r_1} - X_{D,n-r_1}B_{n-r_1}) = O(1).$$

This suggests the following OLS, in which $(I - \boldsymbol{P}(H))$ is inserted in all the products.

$$\hat{B}_{n-r_1} = (X'_{n-r_1}(I - \boldsymbol{P}(H))X_{n-r_1})^{-1}X'_{n-r_1}(I - \boldsymbol{P}(H))X_{r_1}.$$

To develop an asymptotic analysis let $g_h(\tau)$ be the continuous time representation of $(I - \boldsymbol{P}(H))SH$. In fact

$$g_h(\tau) = g(\tau) - \int_0^1 gh'd\tau(\int_0^1 hh'd\tau)^{-1}h(\tau).$$

The continuous time representation of $(I - \boldsymbol{P}(H))X_{D,n-r_1}$ is

$$D_{h,n-r_1}(\tau) = [0, I_{n-r_1}]RQ'g_h(\tau).$$

The series of $\beta' s_t$ is I(0), and its VMA representation is $\beta' C^*(L)\varepsilon_t$ because of (B.2) and (B.4). On the sum of the MA coefficients we assume

Assumption B.5 *The limit, $\beta' \sum_{j=0}^{\infty} C_j^*$, exists.*

This means that $N(B_1)'C^*(1)$ exists.

Proposition B.3 *If* $r_2 = 0$ *and* $r_1 > 0$, $T^{3/2}\,\mathrm{vec}(\hat{B}_{n-r_1} - B_{n-r_1})$ *is asymptotically distributed in the normal distribution with mean zero and the covariance matrix,*

$$N(B_1)'C^*(1)\Lambda C^*(1)'N(B_1) \otimes (\int_0^1 D_{h,n-r_1} D'_{h,n-r_1} d\tau)^{-1}.$$

Any linear hypothesis on B_{n-r_1} can be tested in the conventional way provided that $C^*(1)$, Λ, and $B_\perp Q'$ are consistently estimated. The estimation of $C^*(1)$ will be discussed later.

B.3 Estimation of the VAR, (B.3)

The stochastic part of X, X_S, is generated by VMA, (B.2), or equivalently, VAR, (B.3). What were needed in the previous two Sections B.1 and B.2 are the parameters of (B.2), but we begin with estimation of all parameters of (B.3), i.e., $r_*, \alpha, \beta, \Gamma_1, \ldots, \Gamma_k$, and Λ, except for k, which is assumed to be given. The DGP of X represented in (B.1) and (B.3) is different from that of Johansen et al. (2000) as explained in Section 2.5. Nevertheless their cointegration analyses can be used for our estimation of parameters of (B.3) from the data of X (not X_S), if we are willing to forsake the efficiency of inference that should be expected from the information on the number of common trends, $n - r$, smaller than the number of variables, n. With X, SH, and H in (B.1) define Z, S_{00}, S_{01}, and S_{11} in the same way as in (5.14), (5.16), (5.17), and (5.18). Note that S_{00} is $n \times n$, while S_{11} is $(n+p)\times(n+p)$. The roots of

$$\det[\lambda S_{11} - S_{10} S_{00}^{-1} S_{01}] = 0$$

are denoted as $\hat{\lambda}_1 > \cdots > \hat{\lambda}_n > \hat{\lambda}_{n+1} = \cdots = \hat{\lambda}_{n+p} = 0$.

We can prove the following propositions. (i) $\hat{\lambda}_1, \ldots, \hat{\lambda}_{r_*}$ each converge in probability to positive values, and $\hat{\lambda}_{r_*+1}, \ldots, \hat{\lambda}_n$ are each $O_p(T^{-1})$. (ii) To derive the limiting distribution of $T\hat{\lambda}_i, i = r_* + 1, \ldots, n$ let $g(\tau)$ and $h(\tau)$ be the same as in Sections 5.1 and 5.5, but unlike the notations therein let the $(n - r_*)$-dimensional, standard Brownian motion process be denoted by $W(\tau)$, $1 \geq \tau \geq 0$. Moreover, construct $F(\tau) = [g(\tau)', W(\tau)']'$, $(p + n - r_*) \times 1$, and

$$\tilde{F}(\tau) = F(\tau) - \int_0^1 Fh' d\tau (\int_0^1 hh' d\tau)^{-1} h(\tau).$$

Then $(T\hat{\lambda}_{r_*+1}, \ldots, T\hat{\lambda}_n)$ weakly converges to the descendingly ordered eigenvalues of

$$\int_0^1 dW(\tau)\tilde{F}' d\tau (\int_0^1 \tilde{F}\tilde{F}' d\tau)^{-1} \int_0^1 \tilde{F} dW(\tau)'. \quad \text{(B.9)}$$

The above (i) and (ii) lead to the well known sequential decision rule to determine r_*. (B.9) is what Johansen et al. (2000) use for their cointegration analyses in their model. [(16)]

For a consistent estimate of csp(β), solve

$$(\hat{\lambda}_i S_{11} - S_{10} S_{00}^{-1} S_{01})\hat{v}_i = 0,$$

and partition $\hat{v}_i$ as $[\hat{v}_{id}', \hat{v}_{is}']'$, where $\hat{v}_{id}$ is $p \times 1$, and $\hat{v}_{is}$ is $n \times 1$. Let $\hat{\beta} = [\hat{v}_{is}, \ldots, \hat{v}_{r_* s}]$. Then csp($\hat{\beta}$) converges in probability to csp(β). Consistent estimators of α, Λ, and $\Gamma_1, \ldots, \Gamma_k$ can be derived as follows. Construct

$$\text{est}(\Delta X_{S,-j}) = (I - \boldsymbol{P}(H_{-j}))\Delta X_{-j}, \quad j = 0, \ldots, k,$$

$$\text{est}(X_{S,-1}) = (I - \boldsymbol{P}([H_{-1}, SH_{-1}])X_{-1},$$

and

$$\text{est}(\Delta X_{S,-*}) = [\text{est}(\Delta X_{S,-1}), \ldots, \text{est}(\Delta X_{S,-k})].$$

Run the OLS with est($\Delta X_{S,0}$) as the dependent variable and

$$[\text{est}(X_{S,-1})\hat{\beta}, \text{est}(\Delta X_{S,-*})]$$

as the independent variable. The OLS coefficients matrices are the estimates of α, $\Gamma_1, \ldots, \Gamma_k$, and the residual covariance matrix estimates Λ.

B.4 Estimation of $C(1), \Lambda$, and $C^*(1)$

What we have needed earlier for the inference on B are consistent estimates of $C(1)$, Λ, and $C^*(1)$ in the VMA representation, (B.2). An estimate of Λ has already been obtained. Estimates of $C(1)$ and $C_0^*, C_1^*, \ldots$ can be derived as follows from the relations that express uniquely $C(1)$ and $C_0^*, C_1^*, \ldots$ by the parameters of VAR, (B.3). With $\Gamma(L) = I - \Gamma_1 L - \cdots - \Gamma_k L^k$, Johansen (1991) showed that

$$C(1) = \beta_\perp(\alpha_\perp' \Gamma(1)\beta_\perp)^{-1}\alpha_\perp'.$$ [(17)]

As for $C^*(1)$, let $\Pi(L) = (1 - L)\Gamma(L) - \alpha\beta' L$ so that $\Pi(L)s_t = \varepsilon_t$. An identity,

$$C^*(L)\Pi(L) = I - C(1)\Gamma(L), \tag{B.10}$$

can be proved. $C_0^*, C_1^*, \ldots$ can be determined uniquely by equating the coefficients on the identical powers of L on both sides of (B.10). Thus $C^*(1)$ can be obtained.

B.5 Estimation of $G_* G_*'$

(B.8) contains $G_* G_*'$. In Section 3.1, $[B, \beta]$ has r_1-dimensional column null space spanned by columns of $[G_B', G_\beta']'$, where G_B is $r \times r_1$ and G_β is $r_* \times r_1$. In B.1 of the present appendix G_* is defined from G_B to make $[G_B, G_*]$ be $r \times r$ orthogonal. Let $\hat{B}$, $n \times r$, be the OLS estimate of $N(B)$, i.e., $[I_r, -\hat{B}_{n-r}']'$, and let $\hat{\beta}$, $n \times r_*$ be such that $\mathrm{csp}(\hat{\beta})$ is a consistent estimate of $\mathrm{csp}(\beta)$. Construct

$$[\hat{B}, \hat{\beta}]'[\hat{B}, \hat{\beta}].$$

Arrange its eigenvalues in ascending order, and let the eigenvectors that correspond to the initial r_1 eigenvalues be $[\hat{G}_B', \hat{G}_\beta']'$ where $\hat{G}_B$ is $r \times r_1$ and $\hat{G}_\beta$ is $r_* \times r_1$. $G_* G_*'$ can be consistently estimated by $I_r - \boldsymbol{P}(\hat{G}_B)$.

C Determination of the Co-breaking Rank

The co-breaking and the co-breaking rank have been explained in Section 2.4 on a specific type of structural changes, i.e., slope changes of trends. In the present appendix we shall show that determination of the co-breaking rank can follow essentially the same procedure that the co-trending rank does. The only major difference is that *linear* trends are eliminated from the data, though a number of other minor adaptations are also needed.

In Section 2.4 the notations in Chapter 2 were used. Let us reproduce the explanation of co-breaking rank with the notations in Chapter 4 and thereafter,

$$X_D = SHQB'_\perp + HK + O(1).$$

Q is $p \times (n-r)$, $B'_\perp$ is $(n-r) \times n$, and $\mathrm{rank}(Q) = \mathrm{rank}(B'_\perp) = n - r$. In Chapter 4 and thereafter H and SH are not specialised, but here as well as in Section 2.4 they are specialised into

$$H = [\boldsymbol{\iota}, \boldsymbol{du}(b_1), \ldots, \boldsymbol{du}(b_{p-1})],$$

$$SH = [\boldsymbol{t}, \boldsymbol{dt}(b_1), \ldots, \boldsymbol{dt}(b_{p-1})],$$

defined in the equations (2.4), (2.12), and (2.13), where $\boldsymbol{t} = [1, \ldots, T]'$. Let q'_1 be the first row of Q, and Q_2 be the rest of Q, having $p-1$ rows and $n-r$ columns. Then

$$SHQB'_\perp = \boldsymbol{t}q'_1B'_\perp + [\boldsymbol{dt}(b_1), \ldots, \boldsymbol{dt}(b_{p-1})]Q_2B'_\perp.$$

$Q_2B'_\perp$ in the equation above is identical to P_2 in Section 2.4, and the co-breaking rank is the rank of the column null space of $Q_2B'_\perp$, i.e., $n - \mathrm{rank}(Q_2B'_\perp)$.

C.1 The Number of Common Breaks

We shall call $\mathrm{rank}(Q_2B'_\perp)$ the number of common breaks in analogy to the number of common trends in the co-trending. The following development will focus on the number of common breaks instead of the co-breaking rank. The determination of the former is equivalent to that of the latter. It can be shown that $\text{rank}(Q_2B'_\perp) = \text{rank}(Q_2)$. This is because $B'_\perp$ has its full row rank, $n-r$, by assumption, and Q_2 is $(p-1)\times(n-r)$. Let $n-\tilde{r}$ denote $\text{rank}(Q_2)$. In general $n-\tilde{r} \leq n-r$ by the construction of Q_2 from Q. If $n-\tilde{r} < n-r$, then there exist $\tilde{Q}$, which is $(p-1)\times(n-\tilde{r})$, and $\tilde{B}'_\perp$, which is $(n-\tilde{r})\times n$, such that $Q_2B'_\perp = \tilde{Q}\tilde{B}'_\perp$ and $\text{rank}(\tilde{Q}) = \text{rank}(\tilde{B}_\perp) = n-\tilde{r}$. Thus $\text{rank}(\tilde{Q})$ is the number of common breaks. If $n-r = n-\tilde{r}$, we may write $\tilde{Q} = Q_2, \tilde{B}'_\perp = B'_\perp$, and we have in general

$$SHQB'_\perp = \boldsymbol{t}q'_1B'_\perp + [\boldsymbol{dt}(b_1), \ldots, \boldsymbol{dt}(b_{p-1})]\tilde{Q}\tilde{B}'_\perp.$$

Introducing X_S, the data matrix X is modelled as

$$X = \boldsymbol{t}q'_1B'_\perp + [\boldsymbol{dt}(b_1), \ldots, \boldsymbol{dt}(b_{p-1})]\tilde{Q}\tilde{B}'_\perp + HK + X_S + O(1). \tag{C.1}$$

The assumptions on X_S are identical to those used in dealing with the co-trending.

The role of $B_\perp$ $(n\times(n-r))$ in Chapter 2 is played here by $\tilde{B}_\perp$ $(n\times(n-\tilde{r}))$. The orthogonal complement of $\tilde{B}_\perp$ will be denoted by $\tilde{B}$, which plays the role of B. With the cointegration matrix β, $\tilde{r}_1$ denotes the dimension of the vector space, $\text{csp}(\tilde{B}_1)$, that is common to $\text{csp}(\tilde{B})$ and $\text{csp}(\beta)$. The orthogonal compliment of $\tilde{B}_1$ within $\text{csp}(\tilde{B})$ is denoted by $\text{csp}(\tilde{B}_2)$, and its dimension by $\tilde{r}_2$.

C.2 Detrended Covariance Matrix

When the simple *linear* trends are fitted to X in (C.1), the residual data matrix is

$$\begin{aligned}(I-\boldsymbol{P}([\boldsymbol{\iota},\boldsymbol{t}]))X &= (I-\boldsymbol{P}([\boldsymbol{\iota},\boldsymbol{t}]))[\boldsymbol{dt}(b_1), \ldots, \boldsymbol{dt}(b_{p-1})]\tilde{Q}\tilde{B}'_\perp \\ &\quad + (I-\boldsymbol{P}([\boldsymbol{\iota},\boldsymbol{t}]))HK + (I-\boldsymbol{P}([\boldsymbol{\iota},\boldsymbol{t}]))X_S + O(1),\end{aligned}$$

and the covariance matrix of the residuals is

$$T^{-3}X'(I-\boldsymbol{P}([\boldsymbol{\iota},\boldsymbol{t}]))X. \tag{C.2}$$

Compute n sets of the eigenvalues, eigenvectors, and principal components of (C.2), and order them in the descending order of the eigenvalues indexed as $i = 1, \ldots, n$. The sets for $i = 1, \ldots, n-\tilde{r}$, for $i = n-\tilde{r}+1, \ldots, n-\tilde{r}_1$, and for $i = n-\tilde{r}_1+1, \ldots, n$ have the same properties as those of Group $\perp$, Group 2, and Group 1, respectively, for the co-trending given in Chapter 3. Assuming that $\tilde{B}'_\perp\tilde{B}_\perp = I_{n-\tilde{r}}$, the eigenvectors of

$$\lim_{T\to\infty} T^{-3}\tilde{Q}'[\boldsymbol{dt}(b_1), \ldots, \boldsymbol{dt}(b_{p-1})]'(I-\boldsymbol{P}([\boldsymbol{\iota},\boldsymbol{t}]))[\boldsymbol{dt}(b_1), \ldots, \boldsymbol{dt}(b_{p-1})]\tilde{Q}$$

will be denoted by $\tilde{\eta}_{\perp,i}, i = 1, \ldots, n - \tilde{r}$. It corresponds to $\eta_{\perp,i}$ in Sections 3.2 and 4.1.

In spite of these similarities to the co-trending, the principal components here are not completely identical to those in Chapter 4. A primary difference is due to the fact that $(I - \boldsymbol{P}(\iota))X_S$ in Chapter 4 has to be replaced by $(I - \boldsymbol{P}([\iota, \boldsymbol{t}]))X_S$. Precise specifications of the test statistics for $UURT$, $MURT$, and TRT need to be modified as given in the following three subsections. With such modifications the sequential decision rule in Chapter 7 is applicable to determination of $n-\tilde{r}$, which is the number of common breaks, jointly with $\tilde{r}_2$ and $\tilde{r}_1$.

C.3 *UURT*

$UURT$ has been introduced in Section 5.1 to test for the unit root in the univariate series of x_t. It should be modified for the co-breaking as follows. Z_0 in (5.2) should include $\boldsymbol{t}$ so that

$$Z_0 = [\iota, \boldsymbol{du}(b_1), \ldots, \boldsymbol{du}(b_{p-1}), \boldsymbol{t}, \Delta x_{-1}, \ldots, \Delta x_{-k}].$$

Consequently

$$Z = [\iota, \boldsymbol{du}(b_1), \ldots, \boldsymbol{du}(b_{p-1}), \boldsymbol{t}, \boldsymbol{dt}(b_1), \ldots, \boldsymbol{dt}(b_{p-1}), x_{-1}, \Delta x_{-1}, \ldots, \Delta x_{-k}].$$

With these Z_0 and Z, the expression of $UURT$ in (5.3) need not be changed except for the degrees of freedom in the numerator, i.e.,

$$UURT = [(T - 2k - 2p - 2)^{-1}\Delta x'(I - \boldsymbol{P}(Z))\Delta x]^{-1}[p^{-1}\Delta x'(\boldsymbol{P}(Z) - \boldsymbol{P}(Z_0))\Delta x].$$

The null limiting distribution is constructed as follows. For $j = 1, \ldots, p-1$ define

$$\delta u(\tau, b_j) = \begin{cases} 0 & \text{if } 0 \leq \tau \leq b_j \\ 1 & \text{if } b_j < \tau \leq 1 \end{cases}$$

$$\delta t(\tau, b_j) = \begin{cases} 0 & \text{if } 0 \leq \tau \leq b_j \\ \tau - b_j & \text{if } b_j < \tau \leq 1 \end{cases}$$

and construct

$$\delta u(\tau)' = [\delta u(\tau, b_1), \ldots, \delta u(\tau, b_{p-1})], \tag{C.3}$$

$$\delta t(\tau)' = [\delta t(\tau, b_1), \ldots, \delta t(\tau, b_{p-1})], \tag{C.4}$$

$$mu(\tau)' = [1, \delta u(\tau)', \tau], \tag{C.5}$$

$$mt(\tau)' = [\delta t(\tau)', B_1(\tau)].$$

τ is included in $mu(\tau)$. $B_1(\tau)$ in $mt(\tau)$ is the scalar standard Brownian motion. Finally let

$$\tilde{m}(\tau) = mt(\tau) - \int_0^1 mt(\tau)mu(\tau)'d\tau(\int_0^1 mu(\tau)mu(\tau)'d\tau)^{-1}mu(\tau),$$

and tabulate the distribution of

$$p^{-1}\int_0^1 dB_1(\tau)\tilde{m}(\tau)'(\int_0^1 \tilde{m}(\tau)\tilde{m}(\tau)'d\tau)^{-1}\int_0^1 \tilde{m}(\tau)dB_1(\tau). \qquad \text{(C.6)}$$

In Group $\perp$, i.e., $i = 1, \ldots, n - \tilde{r}$, if $\tilde{B}_\perp\tilde{\eta}_{\perp,i}$ is not a cointegration vector, $UURT$ on the i-th principal component of (C.2) is asymptotically distributed as (C.6). If $\tilde{B}_\perp\tilde{\eta}_{\perp,i}$ is a cointegration vector, $UURT$ on the ith principal component diverges asymptotically. For Group 2, if $\tilde{r}_2 = 1$, $UURT$ on this principal component is asymptotically distributed as (C.6). For Group 1, i.e., $i = n-\tilde{r}_1+1, \ldots, n$, $UURT$ on each individual principal component diverges asymptotically.

C.4 *MURT*

$MURT$ has been introduced in Section 5.5 to test for the zero cointegration rank on the d-dimensional series with the data matrix X. It should be modified for the co-breaking as follows. Z in (5.14) should include $\boldsymbol{t}$ so that

$$Z = [\boldsymbol{\iota}, \boldsymbol{du}(b_1), \ldots, \boldsymbol{du}(b_{p-1}), \boldsymbol{t}, \Delta X_{-1}, \ldots, \Delta X_{-k}]$$

and this Z should be used to construct S_{00}, S_{01}, and S_{11} in (5.15), (5.16), and (5.17). Moreover (5.16) and (5.17) should be modified to

$$S_{01} = (T - k - 1)^{-1}\Delta X'(I - \boldsymbol{P}(Z))[\boldsymbol{dt}(b_1), \ldots, \boldsymbol{dt}(b_{p-1}), X_{-1}],$$

$$S_{11} = (T - k - 1)^{-1}[\boldsymbol{dt}(b_1), \ldots, \boldsymbol{dt}(b_{p-1}), X_{-1}]'(I - \boldsymbol{P}(Z)) \times [\boldsymbol{dt}(b_1), \ldots, \boldsymbol{dt}(b_{p-1}), X_{-1}].$$

With these modified S_{00}, S_{01}, and S_{11} the expression for $MURT$ is identical to (5.15). The null limiting distribution is constructed with $mu(\tau)$ in (C.5) and

$$Mt(\tau)' = [\delta t(\tau)', B_d(\tau)'],$$

where $B_d(\tau)'$ is the d-dimensional, row-vector of standard Brownian motion. Let

$$\tilde{M}(\tau) = Mt(\tau) - \int_0^1 Mt(\tau)mu(\tau)'d\tau(\int_0^1 mu(\tau)mu(\tau)'d\tau)^{-1}mu(\tau).$$

The limiting distribution is

$$\int_0^1 dB_d(\tau)\tilde{M}(\tau)'(\int_0^1 \tilde{M}(\tau)\tilde{M}(\tau)'d\tau)^{-1}\int_0^1 \tilde{M}(\tau)dB_d(\tau)'. \tag{C.7}$$

If $\tilde{r}_2 \geq 2$ in Group 2, the above X is $\tilde{r}_2$ principal components of (C.1) for $i = n-r+1, \ldots, n-\tilde{r}_1$, and $d = \tilde{r}_2$. $MURT$ is asymptotically distributed as (C.7), and the limiting distribution of the maximum eigenvalue of $MURT$ is the distribution of the maximum eigenvalue of (C.7).

C.5 *TRT*

TRT in Section 6.3 used the demeaned $[H, SH]$. Here it should be replaced by the residuals in the regression of $[H, SH]$ on the linear trends, i.e.,

$$(I - \boldsymbol{P}([\boldsymbol{\iota}, \boldsymbol{t}])[\boldsymbol{du}(b_1), \ldots, \boldsymbol{du}(b_{p-1}), \boldsymbol{dt}(b_1), \ldots, \boldsymbol{dt}(b_{p-1})].$$

With this modification the expression, (6.2), remains unchanged for the data, Z, of the d-dimensional series. The limiting distribution is constructed as follows. Apply the demeaning and the linear detrending operations in the continuous time to $\delta u(\tau)$, $\delta t(\tau)$, and $B_d(\tau)$. Let $\tilde{\delta} u(\tau), \tilde{\delta} t(\tau)$, and $\tilde{B}_d(\tau)$ denote the results. In mathematical expressions,

$$\delta(\tau) = [\delta u(\tau)', \delta t(\tau)', B_d(\tau)']',$$

and

$$\tilde{\delta}(\tau) = [\tilde{\delta} u(\tau)', \tilde{\delta} t(\tau)', \tilde{B}_d(\tau)']'$$

are related by

$$\tilde{\delta}(\tau) = \delta(\tau) - \int_0^1 \delta(\tau)d\tau - 12(\tau - (1/2))\int_0^1 (\tau - (1/2))\delta(\tau)d\tau.$$

V_0, V_1, and V_2 in (6.4), (6.5), and (6.6) are replaced by

$$\tilde{V}_0 = \int_0^1 \tilde{B}_d(\tau)\tilde{B}_d(\tau)'d\tau,$$

$$\tilde{V}_1 = \int_0^1 \tilde{B}_d(\tau)[\tilde{\delta} u(\tau)', \tilde{\delta} t(\tau)']d\tau(\int_0^1 [\tilde{\delta} u(\tau)', \tilde{\delta} t(\tau)']'[\tilde{\delta} u(\tau)', \tilde{\delta} t(\tau)']d\tau)^{-1}$$
$$\times \int_0^1 [\tilde{\delta} u(\tau)', \tilde{\delta} t(\tau)']'\tilde{B}_d(\tau)'d\tau,$$

and

$$\tilde{V}_2 = \int_0^1 \tilde{B}_d(\tau)\tilde{\delta}t(\tau)'\tilde{Q}d\tau(\int_0^1 \tilde{Q}'\tilde{\delta}t(\tau)\tilde{\delta}t(\tau)'\tilde{Q}d\tau)^{-1}\int_0^1 \tilde{Q}'\tilde{\delta}t(\tau)\tilde{B}_d(\tau)'d\tau.$$

The limiting distribution is given by

$$(\tilde{V}_0 - \tilde{V}_1)^{-1/2}(\tilde{V}_1 - \tilde{V}_2)(\tilde{V}_0 - \tilde{V}_1)'^{-1/2}. \tag{C.8}$$

When Z is the principal components in Group 2 so that $d = \tilde{r}_2$, TRT is asymptotically distributed as (C.8). On the other hand TRT diverges asymptotically when Z is an individual principal component in Group $\perp$.

As for the unknown parameter, $\tilde{Q}$, we should use the reduced rank regression of $(I - P([\iota, t]))X$ upon $(I - \boldsymbol{P}([\iota, t]))[\boldsymbol{dt}(b_1), \ldots, \boldsymbol{dt}(b_{p-1})]$. The rank for the regression should be chosen in the context of testing each grouping method as explained in Section 6.7.

Notes

(1) Suppose that n variables share the same break points, $[Tb_1], \ldots, [Tb_m]$ so that we have $(m+1)$ elementary trend functions, $[\boldsymbol{t}, \boldsymbol{dt}(b_1), \ldots, \boldsymbol{dt}(b_m)]$, where $\boldsymbol{dt}(b_j)$ is defined in (2.13). $p = m + 1$. If $m < n$, we have $ctmax = p \leq n$. If $m \geq n$, we have $p > ctmax = n$.

(2) The ideas, co-trending and co-breaking, have been presented in Hatanaka (1998) independently of Hendry and Mizon (1998), though neither of the words was used.

(3) In Johansen et al. (2000) the whole sample period is divided into q sub-sample periods. In its $H_l(r)$ the trend is linear, but intercepts and slopes may differ among sub-sample periods. Our model of trends is such that discontinuous step changes do not occur at break points. If this difference is adjusted, their model of trends is equivalent to the case of ours with q elementary functions, $[\boldsymbol{\iota}, \boldsymbol{du}(b_1), \ldots, \boldsymbol{du}(b_{q-1})]$. The trend in the j-th sub-sample period is $\tau_{l,j}t$ in their equation (2.8) inheriting the property of τ_1 from Johansen (1994). It is easy to derive that the number of common trends in the *entire sample periods* is equal to the rank of $[\tau_{l,1}, \ldots, \tau_{l,q}]$, which is $p \times q$. (p is the number of variables.)

(4) Regarding non-uniqueness of eigenvectors, we mean that the two eigenvectors can be chosen so that the relevant statement holds.

(5) $T^{-2}B_2X_SX_SB_2 - W_{22}$ being $O_p(T^{-1/2})$ is a theoretical result, rather than an assumption, derived from Assumption 3.1.

(6) Hatanaka (2000) dealt with the model in which the order of trends may be higher than $O(T^{3/2})$ but the relations among trends hold exactly. In this book the trends are $O(T^{3/2})$ but the residuals in $O(T^{1/2})$ are admitted. Between the two models the limit expressions of the eigenvalues in groups $\perp$ and 2 are identical if the orders of trends are identical.

(7) $(p+1)^{-1}$ may be eliminated from (5.3) and (5.7) simultaneously.

(8) A stationary process is indeterministic if the prediction error cannot be made zero in the optimal prediction of x_t from $x_{t-1}, x_{t-2}, \ldots$.

(9) The univariate version of $(T-k-1)S_{01}S_{11}^{-1}S_{10}$ is the numerator of (5.3) multiplied by $(p+1)$, i.e.,

$$\Delta x'(P(Z) - P(Z_0))\Delta x = \Delta x'(I - P(Z_0))Z_* \times (Z_*'(I - P(Z_0))Z_*)^{-1}Z_*'(I - P(Z_0))\Delta x,$$

where $Z_* = [SH, x_{-1}]$, because Z in (5.14) was written Z_0 in (5.2). The univariate version of S_{00} would be asymptotically equal to the denominator of (5.3) even if we do not modify the denominator of $UURT$ as mentioned in the text.

(10) We have attempted to compare the differenced series of principal components, (4.7) and (4.11), in the framework of a regression model concerning the significance of the term, $HQ\eta_{\perp,i}$, in (4.7). The covariance matrix of the error term is asymptotically singular. A known method to deal with the singularity has been found to lack reasonably good finite sample property.

(11) $T^{1/2}(\tilde{\lambda}_{n-r} - 1)$ is $O_p(1)$, while $T^{1/2}(\tilde{\lambda}_{n-r+1} - 1)$ diverges to $-\infty$ as $T \to \infty$. This does not seem useful for determination of $n-r$ because the limit distribution of $T^{1/2}(\tilde{\lambda}_{n-r} - 1)$ is difficult to derive.

(12) It can be shown that if $q \geq n-r$, $\hat{Q}_{(q)}\hat{R}'_{(q)} \xrightarrow{p} QR'$.

(13) If $\lambda_i(G_{\perp\perp})$ is a root with multiplicity, η_i can be chosen so that $\hat{\eta}_i - \eta_i$ is $O_p(T^{-1/2})$. See Note (4) above.

(14) A comment on the maximum likelihood approach may be desired. The likelihood function can be easily derived for the parameterisation on the deterministic part by $QB'_\perp$ and K given in Section 4 (in addition to those in (B.2)). The likelihood function for B has to be indirectly derived from it. Given r, the likelihood function can be maximised only through iterations. We have judged the approach impractical. However our theoretical analyses of the scores have indicated the necessity to distinguish B_1 and B_2 in Section 3.1 of the text.

(15) Assuming that $r_2 > 0$ and $r_1 > 0$, partition X as $[X_{r_1}, X_{r_2}, X_{n-r}]$. An alternative to $\hat{B}_{n-r}$ in the text is to run the OLS with X_{r_1} as the dependent variable and $[X_{r_2}, X_{n-r}]$ as the independent variable. Partitioning $X_{D\perp}$ as $[X_{D\perp,r_1}, X_{D\perp,r_2}, X_{D\perp,n-r}]$, it is seen that $X_{D\perp,r_2}$ is in csp$(X_{D\perp,n-r})$. Therefore, this OLS has to be run in the context of asymptotic multicollinearity among the independent variables. Moreover, X_{r_1} must be chosen so that X_{S,r_1} is I(0) if we wish to make this OLS fill in the vacuum on $B_{n-r}G_B$ made in the inference by $\hat{B}_{n-r}$.

(16) They further rewrite (B.9), and propose approximation to it by the Gamma distribution.

(17) See Johansen (1995, p.95) for the calculation of $\alpha_{\perp}$ and $\beta_{\perp}$.

References

1. Bai, J., Lumsdaine, R.L., Stock, J.H. (1998) Testing for and dating common breaks in multivariate time series. Review of Economic Studies, **65**, 395–432.
2. Clements, M.P., Hendry, D.F. (1999) Forecasting Nonstationary Economic Time Series. MIT Press, Cambridge.
3. Dickey, D.A., Fuller, W.A. (1979) Distribution of the estimators for autoregressive time series with a unit root. Journal of the American Statistical Association, **74**, 427–431.
4. Elliott, G., Rothenberg, T.J., Stock, J.H. (1996) Efficient tests for an autoregressive unit root. Econometrica, **64**, 813–836.
5. Engle, R.F., Granger C.W.J. (1987) Co-integration and error correction: representation, estimation, and testing. Econometrica, **55**, 251–276.
6. Granger, C.W.J. (1981) Some properties of time series data and their use in econometric model specification. Journal of Econometrics, **16**, 121-130.
7. Granger, C.W.J. (1986) Developments in the study of cointegrated economics variables. Oxford Bulletin of Economics and Statistics, **48**, 213-228.
8. Granger, C.W.J. (1988) Models that generate trends. Journal of Time Series Analysis, **9**, 329-343.
9. Hatanaka, M. (1998) Reorientation of the time series analyses for macroeconomics. Japanese Economic Review, **49**, 1–16.
10. Hatanaka, M. (2000) How to determine the number of relations among deterministic trends. Japanese Economic Review, **51**, 349–374.
11. Hendry, D.F., Mizon, G.E. (1998) Exogeneity, causality, and co-breaking in economic policy analysis of a small econometric model of money in the UK. Empirical Economics, **23**, 267-294.
12. Inoue, A. (1999) Tests of cointegration rank with a trend break. Journal of Econometrics, **90**, 215–237.
13. Johansen, S. (1988) Statistical analysis of cointegration vectors. Journal of Economic Dynamics and Control, **12**, 231–254.
14. Johansen, S. (1991) Estimation and hypothesis testing of cointegration vectors in Gaussian vector autoregressive model. Econometrica, **59**, 1551–1580.
15. Johansen, S. (1994) The role of the constant term in cointegration analysis of nonstationary variables. Econometric Reviews, **13**, 205–219.
16. Johansen S. (1995) Likelihood-Based Inference in Cointegrated Vector Autoregressive Models. Oxford University Press, Oxford.
17. Johansen, S., Mosconi R., Nielsen B. (2000) Cointegration analysis in the presence of structural breaks in the deterministic trend. Econometrics Journal, **3**, 216–249.
18. Klein, L.R., Kosobud, R.F. (1961) Some econometrics of growth: great ratios of economics. Quarterly Journal of Economics, **75**, 173–198.

19. Kunitomo, N. (1996) Structural changes in the unit root and cointegration hypotheses with application to macroeconomic time series. Kinyu Kenkyu, **15**, 1–43, Bank of Japan.
20. Ng, S., P. Perron, P. (1995) Unit root tests in ARMA models with data-dependent methods for the selection of the truncation lag. Journal of the American Statistical Association, **90**, 268–281.
21. Ogaki, M., Park, J.Y. (1998) A cointegration approach to estimating preference parameters. Journal of Econometrics, **82**, 107–134.
22. Perron, P. (1989) The great crash, the oil price shock, and the unit root hypothesis. Econometrica, **57**, 1361–1401.
23. Said, S.E., Dickey, D.A. (1984) Testing for unit roots in autoregressive-moving average models of unknown order. Biometrika, **71**, 599–607.
24. Schmidt, P., Phillips, P.C.B. (1992) LM tests for a unit root in the presence of deterministic trends. Oxford Bulletin of Economics and Statistics, **54**, 257–287.
25. Toda, H.Y. (1994) Finite sample properties of likelihood ratio tests for cointegrating ranks when linear trends are present. Review of Economics and Statistics, **76**, 66–79.
26. Yamada, K., Hatanaka, M., (2002) The long run neutrality of money in Japan. mimeographed.

MIX
Papier aus verantwortungsvollen Quellen
Paper from responsible sources
FSC® C105338

If you have any concerns about our products,
you can contact us on
ProductSafety@springernature.com

In case Publisher is established outside the EU,
the EU authorized representative is:
Springer Nature Customer Service Center GmbH
Europaplatz 3, 69115 Heidelberg, Germany

Printed by Libri Plureos GmbH
in Hamburg, Germany